Shakespeare
and his
Contemporaries
Charles Nicholl

Published in Great Britain by National Portrait Gallery Publications,
National Portrait Gallery, St Martin's Place, London WC2H 0HE

For a complete catalogue of current publications please write to the
address above, or visit our website at www.npg.org.uk/publications

First published 2005
This edition published 2015
Copyright © National Portrait Gallery, 2005, 2015
Text copyright © Charles Nicholl, 2005, 2015

ISBN 978 1 85514 580 1

A catalogue record for this book is available from the British Library.

10 9 8 7 6 5 4 3 2 1

Managing Editor: Christopher Tinker
Editors: Susie Foster, Andrew Roff
Design: Smith & Gilmour
Production: Ruth Müller-Wirth, Kathleen Bloomfield
Printed and bound in China

Every purchase supports the National Portrait Gallery, London

Contents

To the Reader.

This Figure, that thou here feeſt put,
    It was for gentle Shakeſpeare cut;
Wherein the Grauer had a ſtrife
    with Nature, to out-doo the life :
O, could he but haue drawne his wit
    As well in braſſe, as he hath hit
Hisface ; the Print would then ſurpaſſe
    All, that was euer writ in braſſe.
But, ſince he cannot, Reader, looke
    Not on his Picture, but his Booke.

                      B. I.

Introduction

'Reader,' advises Ben Jonson, 'look not on his picture, but
his book.' He is right, of course. The book he is referring to is
the First Folio edition of Shakespeare's plays, and the picture
is the rather bland engraving of the author by Martin Droeshout
that forms its frontispiece. Yet the picture continues to hold our
attention; we do not stop looking on it. It is little more than an
incised sketch, a naïve-seeming icon, but somewhere behind that
familiar mask – the stiff collar, the domed head, the perfunctory
beard – is the face of Shakespeare.

Fortunately, other portraits in this gallery of Elizabethan
and Jacobean writers tell us more than Droeshout's notoriously
reticent image of Shakespeare (and fortunately we know of other,
more compelling images of Shakespeare too). These pictures
are not often intimate – the overall style is formal – but they
are full of physical presence and detail: John Donne's raffishly
tilted hat; the thin-lipped smile of the wit John Harington; the
pamphleteer Thomas Nashe in leg-irons; Sir Walter Ralegh
beside his eight-year-old son, who will later die in search of
gold in South America. The portraits show us these people
vividly foregrounded, but there is seldom much in the way of
background. We see faces and figures in an undefined setting:
behind them mere shadow, indistinctness, at most a swathe of
curtain. To provide something of that background – the physical
and cultural landscape in which Shakespeare and his

....
OPPOSITE
William Shakespeare
Martin Droeshout, 1632 or 1663–4
This iconic image from the First Folio is thought to be based
on a lost picture showing 'gentle Shakespeare' in his forties.

contemporaries lived and wrote – is broadly the purpose of this introduction.

Shakespeare's literary career covers a quarter of a century, from his shadowy beginnings in the late 1580s to his last datable work, *Henry VIII*, performed at the Globe theatre in 1613. Like many of the authors in this book, he is both Elizabethan and Jacobean, and in his riddling 'dark comedies' of the early seventeenth century one senses the uneasy transition between the two. They seem to us now rather different periods. We think of the Elizabethan Age as a time of national invigoration, a heady era of patriotism and poetry, while the accession of James I in 1603 seems to usher in a more sophisticated, cynical, corrupt air. One of the differences, certainly, lay in the Queen's attitude to her subjects. 'I believe no prince living,' wrote the memoirist Sir Robert Naunton some thirty years after her death, 'that was so great a courter of her people, yea of the commons, and that stooped and descended lower in presenting her person to the public view as she passed in her progresses and perambulations.' Elizabeth had lived through dark days as a princess: the execution of her mother, Anne Boleyn; the years of virtual house-arrest during the reign of her Catholic half-sister, Mary. She understood deeply that 'the strength of her kingdom … rested in the love and fidelity of her people'.

That the Queen inspired great devotion in her subjects is not in doubt, but one should not translate this into a sentimental idea,

....

OPPOSITE
Elizabeth I
Marcus Gheeraerts the Younger, c.1592
The 'Ditchley' portrait was probably commissioned by Sir Henry Lee on the occasion of the Queen's visit to Ditchley Park, Oxfordshire, in 1592. She stands on a globe, presiding magnificently over England. Above her (as the partly legible sonnet on the right of the painting explains) the sun represents her glory and the thunder her power.

....
Sir Robert Dudley, 1st Earl of Leicester
Unknown artist, late eighteenth
or nineteenth century
Robert Dudley had known Queen
Elizabeth since childhood, and was
her prime court favourite for many
years. This marble bust shows
Leicester in his mid-fifties, following
his service as military commander
in the Netherlands.

popular in fictional treatments, of Shakespeare exchanging
jovial banter with her. Courtly poets such as Ralegh and
Harington and the Earl of Oxford may have done so, but
Shakespeare was a mere 'play-maker', and his personal contact
with the Queen was probably limited. He was the paid entertainer
whose shows were put on at court; he was a member of the Lord
Chamberlain's troupe, thus a servant of one of her servants.
There is a tradition that the *Merry Wives of Windsor* was a royal
commission, that the Queen had a desire to see 'Falstaff in love',
but this story is first heard in the eighteenth century and is of
dubious authenticity. *Henry VIII* ends gracefully with the birth
of Elizabeth, 'this royal infant', who:

> Though in her cradle, yet now promises
> Upon this land a thousand thousand blessings
> Which time shall bring to ripeness.

It would be nice to think Shakespeare paid this tribute to the Queen in the last scene of his last play, but the lines were probably written by the play's co-author, John Fletcher.

Elizabeth exploited a cultish idea of devotion, which her unmarried status undoubtedly fuelled. She was the 'Virgin Queen' hymned by poets under such symbolic names as Gloriana and Astraea. Her court simmered with an eroticised sense of service. Around her ranged the brilliant array of her favourites, with whom she conducted long-running, coquettish, hot-and-cold affairs. The first (whom she perhaps loved more deeply than any other) was Robert Dudley, Earl of Leicester. Enemies characterised him as a Machiavellian schemer whose courtship of Elizabeth showed 'how desirous he hath been of a kingdom'; this is the theme of the Catholic pamphlet *Leicester's Commonwealth*, smuggled into England in the early 1580s. The mysterious death of his first wife, Amy Robsart, fuelled the rumours. Elizabeth's affections also lighted on Sir Christopher Hatton, her dandified Lord Chancellor (centuries later dismissed somewhat unfairly by Lytton Strachey: 'Hatton danced, and that is all we know of him'), and on Sir Walter Ralegh, a young adventurer and soldier in 1582, when he became her Captain of the Guard. Ralegh was her confidant and amorous sparring-partner for ten years, but was furiously rusticated when he secretly married one of her Maids of Honour. The last of the royal entanglements was with Robert Devereux, 2nd Earl of Essex. Tall, brash, handsome and impetuous, he alternately enraged and besotted her. The end of the affair was more dramatic than any: Essex was beheaded on Tower Hill in the spring of 1601, after the abortive coup known as the Essex Rising.

While these high-profile paramours rose and fell, Elizabeth's political ministers piloted the ship of state more

....

Robert Devereux, 2nd Earl of Essex
Nicholas Hilliard, c.1595

The Earl of Essex, the last of the ageing Queen's favourites, is seen here as a tall, dashing young cavalier. Shortly before the 1601 rebellion that cost him his head, his supporters commissioned a performance of Shakespeare's *Richard II*, complete with the controversial deposition scene (excised from printed editions of the play). The Queen understood the message, saying: 'I am Richard II, know ye not that?'

SERO, SED SERIO

Robert Cecil, 1st Earl of Salisbury
John de Critz the Elder, 1602

The features are a stereotype, but the details of de Critz's portrait add an air of busy bureaucratic efficiency. The dispatches and seal-bag on the desk relate to Cecil's position as Elizabeth's Secretary of State. The motto SERO SED SERIO – 'late but in earnest' – is usually associated with tardy repentance, but here suggests the political skills of patience and decisiveness. The portrait was painted shortly before the accession of James, which Cecil did so much to engineer.

cautiously. Her most trusted advisers were Lord Burghley, the Treasurer, and the more hawkish Sir Francis Walsingham, Secretary of State and the great Elizabethan spymaster. These loyal bureaucrats were experts in the art of survival. Burghley's motto, 'Prudens qui patiens' – 'The prudent man waits patiently' – expresses this well, and none was more proficient in the art than his sickly, brilliant son, Sir Robert Cecil, who served as Elizabeth's Secretary of State from 1596 and rose to become James's chief minister, before his death in 1612, at the age of about fifty.

It was an age of spectacle and slightly ersatz chivalry. One writer came almost to symbolise this revived chivalric ethos:

....

The funeral cortège of Sir Philip Sidney
Theodor de Bry, 1587
This is one of thirty-two engravings of Sidney's funeral procession from Thomas Lant's *Sequitur celebritas et pompa funebris*. When pasted together horizontally they depict a procession of 344 figures. The early biographer John Aubrey saw them thus, as a child, in the parlour of Mr Singleton of Gloucester, making 'such a strong impression on my tender phantasy that I remember it as if it were but yesterday.'

Sir Henry Lee
Antonis Mor, 1568
Courtier, poet, art-collector and instigator of the Accession Day tilts, Lee is shown here in elegantly understated black and white. The painting is a little earlier than the first of the tilts (c.1571), but their ethos is suggested by the rings worn like chivalric favours, and the armillary spheres embroidered on his sleeve are symbols of celestial harmony.

the young soldier-poet Sir Philip Sidney, nephew of the Earl of Leicester and son-in-law of Sir Francis Walsingham. His heroic death in the Netherlands, at the age of thirty-two, occasioned an outpouring of elegies and a sumptuous funeral procession, held in London on 16 February 1587. Also part of this chivalric spin were the Accession Day tilts, held every 17 November to commemorate the Queen's accession to the throne. Noblemen, knights and aspirant young gallants jousted for her favours, and poets such as George Peele (in *Polyhymnia*, 1589) celebrated

....

A *Star* (above) and *Atalanta* (above right)
Inigo Jones
Jones's lively, delicate costume designs show (above left) a figure from *The Lords' Masque* by Thomas Campion, performed at Whitehall on 14 February 1613 to celebrate the wedding of King James's daughter Elizabeth; and (above right) fleet-footed Atalanta from *The Masque of Queens* (1610). A manuscript note identifies the latter as Alathea Talbot, Countess of Arundel, and indicates a colour scheme for her costume of crimson, yellow and white.

their achievements. The Queen's 'champion' in the tilts for many years was Sir Henry Lee, himself an occasional poet. Another was the Earl of Cumberland, his armour dashingly engraved with astrological and alchemical symbols.

The writers supplied this desire for spectacle with increasingly lavish pageants, entertainments and masques. The Earl of Leicester treated the Queen to an aquatic fantasia, with poetry by George Gascoigne and others, at Kenilworth in July 1575; it is optimistically conjectured that the glover John

Sir Henry Unton (detail)
Unknown artist, c.1596
A consort of musicians playing lutes, viols, fiddle and fife, and a procession of masquers in spangled costumes entertain the guests at an Elizabethan wedding feast.

Shakespeare from nearby Stratford-upon-Avon took his eleven-year-old son to see it. The fashion for elaborate court masques reached its heyday under James, with such works as Ben Jonson's *Masque of Blackness* and *Masque of Beauty*. The master of costume and setting for these shows was the flamboyant architect Inigo Jones. Music and dance also flourished, with a string of superb composers such as John Dowland, Thomas Morley, Thomas Campion and Robert Johnson (Johnson's settings for the songs in Shakespeare's *Tempest* survive), but curiously we know of no individual portraits of these musicians.

The writers of the Elizabethan Age expressed a surge of national confidence. They were in a sense its propagandists; in their work the very language quickens with new possibilities. But there was another Elizabethan mood entirely, which they also expressed: it was compounded of scepticism, a sense of transience and a generous dash of that other much-cultivated Elizabethan attribute, melancholy. It is this mix of zest and doubt that makes the period so fascinating. 'I can suck melancholy out of a song as a weasel sucks eggs,' says the embittered humorist Jaques in Shakespeare's *As You Like It* (c.1599), and indeed a sense of melancholy is glimpsed in the writers' portraits. There is not much sense of swashbuckling; cries of 'Gadzooks!' do not spring to mind. There is colour and finery, but the brilliance is somehow sombre; the swagger tinged with introspection. This is partly

....
OPPOSITE
Henry Percy, 9th Earl of Northumberland
Nicholas Hilliard, c.1595
This intriguing miniature shows the Earl around the age of thirty, languid and melancholy.
He is seen, like the distracted Hamlet, 'with his doublet all unbraced,/ No hat upon his head'.
The weighty looking book beside him, and the mathematical conundrum in the background,
suggest a malaise more philosophical than lovelorn.

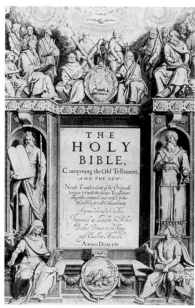

a matter of portrait conventions – a certain sternness was *de rigueur* – but the mood is nonetheless pervasive.

Typical of the young noblemen who catch this note of mental restlessness was Henry Percy, 9th Earl of Northumberland. A close friend of Ralegh, a patron of scientists such as Thomas Harriot and Walter Warner, he was associated with the forbidden fascinations of the occult and was nicknamed the 'Wizard Earl'. Among the poets who sought his patronage was the brilliant Christopher Marlowe, whose play *Dr Faustus* (c.1588) articulates the dangerous thrill of knowledge liberated from theological constraints:

James I of England and VI of Scotland
Early seventeenth century after a portrait
by John de Critz the Elder of c.1606
Some of the contradictions of King James
are caught in this pale, pinch-faced, oddly
unflattering portrait. He was, wrote the
Whig historian Macaulay, 'made up of
two men – a witty, well-read scholar who
wrote, disputed and harangued; and a
nervous, drivelling idiot, who acted'.

Divinity, adieu!
These metaphysics of magicians
And necromantic books are heavenly!
Lines, circles, schemes, letters and characters:
Ay, these are those that Faustus most desires ... .
All things that move between the quiet poles
Shall be at my command ... .

These dramatic rejections of orthodoxy shade into a late
Elizabethan malaise whose classic expression is Shakespeare's
Hamlet (c.1600), with its moody, faltering, doubt-ridden prince,
and his 'craven scruple of thinking too precisely', and his sense
of 'something rotten' in the body politic. Hamlet's mood of
questioning, of nervy unrest, conveys a kind of philosophical
vertigo in an age of rapid transition. It is perhaps this darker

flip-side that speaks to us today, and that brings these authors close to ourselves and our preoccupations. However, one should not forget the tremendous depth and power of religious writing in the period – the sermons of Lancelot Andrewes and John Donne; the Catholic poetry of Henry Constable and Robert Southwell; and, of course, the Authorised Version of the Bible, a revision of William Tyndale's translation that occupied a committee of forty-seven scholars and divines over a period of nearly four years and was issued in 1611.

The King James Bible is a tribute to that monarch, who assiduously promoted it, but it can hardly be called typical of the Jacobean era, whose brittle and cynical tone is more aptly

OPPOSITE

George Villiers, 1st Duke of Buckingham
attributed to William Larkin, c.1616
The shapely attractions of George Villiers, or 'Steenie' as King James called him, are on show in this portrait. From the ostrich-plumes of his hat to the pom-poms of his high-heeled shoes he is the Jacobean peacock exemplified. His political skills were far less splendid, and few tears were shed when Villiers was assassinated by a discontented soldier in 1628.

RIGHT

Robert Carr, Earl of Somerset
Nicholas Hilliard, c.1611
Robert Carr or Ker arrived in England in 1603 as a young Scottish page in James's retinue. 'Strong-shouldered and smooth-faced', his mignon charms were rewarded with lands (including the sequestered estates of Sir Walter Ralegh) and titles (Viscount Rochester and Earl of Somerset). He was eventually found guilty of murdering Sir Thomas Overbury but received a royal pardon in 1624.

characterised by grim Jacobean pyscho-dramas such as John Webster's *Duchess of Malfi* and John Ford's *'Tis Pity She's a Whore*. King James himself combined intellectual acumen, unsavoury personal hygiene and a strong vein of homosexuality. He was married, not unhappily, to the Danish-born Queen Anne, and fathered several children, including the future Charles I, but his preferences lay the other way, and launched a series of empty-headed young mignons to positions of enormous power. Among the dimmest, prettiest and most powerful was George Villiers, 1st Duke of Buckingham. Another of these 'wealthy curlèd darlings' was Robert Carr, Earl of Somerset. In a scandal that cast a pall over the Jacobean court in 1613, Carr was deeply implicated in the murder of his former confidant Sir Thomas Overbury, who opposed his marriage to the voluptuous Frances Howard, but he was for some years shielded from prosecution while more minor abettors went to the gallows.

Another corruption that rankled was James's indiscriminate sale of knighthoods and monopolies to swell the royal coffers. In one four-month period of profitable largesse he bestowed over 900 knighthoods. A stage-comedy called *Eastward Ho!* has a joke about this: 'I ken the man weel,' says a character in a cod Scottish accent, 'he's one of my thirty pound knights.' This insolence earned the authors, Ben Jonson and George Chapman, a spell in prison and the threat of worse: 'the report was that they should then have their ears cut, and noses'. This was in 1605, not the best year to be nibbling at royal prerogatives – the year of the Powder Treason, or Gunpowder Plot, an attempted coup by desperate Catholics whose hopes of toleration, expediently promised by James before his succession, had proved illusory. The story is famous – it was instantly propagandised in pamphlets and ballads: the discovery, in the early hours of 5 November, of thirty-six barrels of gunpowder

CONCILIVM SEPTEM NOBILIVM ANGLORVM CONIVRANTIVM IN NECEM IACOBI · I ·
MAGNÆ · BRITANNIÆ · REGIS · TOTIVSQ · ANGLICI · CONVOCATI · PARLEMENTI ·

Robert
Winter

Christopher
Wright

Iohn
Wright

Thomas
Percy

Guido
Fawkes

Robert
Catesby

Thomas
Winter

Bates

....
The Gunpowder Plot Conspirators, 1605
Published by Crispijn de Passe the Elder, c.1605
Eight of the thirteen conspirators are shown in this contemporary Dutch print. Though unlikely
to be true portraits, the huddled grouping, the tall hats and the decisive gestures are very dramatic.
Robin Catesby, second from the right, was the ringleader; Thomas Percy was a cousin of the Earl
of Northumberland; the hatless figure on the left is Thomas Bates, Catesby's servant.

in the cellars of the Houses of Parliament; the efficient rounding-up of the conspirators in the Midlands; the rhetoric of divine deliverance; the show trials and the public dismemberments. The man arrested in charge of the gunpowder gave his name as John Johnson, but he was soon identified as one Guy or Guido Fawkes, a 32-year-old Catholic from York who had fought in the Low Countries. Among the grimmest documents of the period is the series of confessions extracted from Fawkes in the days after his capture: the deterioration of his signatures, to the last quavering scrawl, testifies to the tortures he was undergoing.

These are some aspects of the courtly world in which Shakespeare and his contemporaries operated, to which they perforce aspired – a glittery but somewhat claustrophobic world in which were mingled idealism and cynicism, lavish spectacle and existentialist speculation, chivalric games and savage executions. But the court is only part of their landscape. For many – the dramatists, certainly, and also the more populist poets and pamphleteers – the centre of their professional life was increasingly the city rather than the court. The city, specifically London, was their habitat: they passed the time together in taverns and theatrical back rooms, and among the booksellers' stalls of St Paul's Churchyard. And as the idea dawns of a

. . . .
ABOVE AND LEFT

Panoramic view of London (with detail of the Globe Theatre)

Claes Jan Visscher, printed c.1615

Visscher's superb panorama shows us Elizabethan London. Though printed in c.1615, certain details suggest it was modelled on drawings done around the turn of the century. The banner of the royal barge shows Tudor rather than Stuart arms, and there is no sign of Salisbury House, which was nearing completion in 1602.

commercial literature – of writing as a trade and livelihood – the city also becomes their market.

London was a city of about 200,000, hungrily expanding into the surrounding countryside. 'London, flower of cities all' was the traditional ditty, though the pamphleteer Nashe phrased it somewhat differently: 'London, thou art the seeded garden of sin, the sea that sucks in all the scummy channels of the realm.' In his *Survey of London* (1598), the great topographer John Stow grumbled about the sprawl: a warren of 'poor cottages' and 'alleys backward' where there were once open fields. The suburbs of Middlesex, complained the Privy Council in 1596, were infested with 'alehouses, taverns, garden-houses converted into dwellings, ordinaries [restaurants], dicing-houses, bowling alleys and brothel-houses'. One of the areas thus described lay between Bishopsgate and Shoreditch – precisely where the writers clustered, close to the first theatres: the *quartier Latin* of Elizabethan London.

For the dramatists, performance at court was a prestigious perk; what counted more were the day's takings in the public theatres – the Theatre and the Curtain in Shoreditch; the Rose, the Globe and the Swan on the Bankside south of the Thames. All these stood outside the city walls, in the so-called 'liberties' beyond the control of the mayor and his aldermen. Their increasing commercial success was often viewed as a civic nuisance – a potential for riotous assembly, for prostitution and pickpocketing, for the transmission of infectious diseases and (no less dangerous) of dissident ideas. They were closely policed by the government and were frequently shut down, usually on health grounds. All play-scripts had to be submitted to the censor. The manuscript of *Sir Thomas More* survives with the censor's annotation: 'Leave out the insurrection wholly & the cause thereof.' Other plays with seditious overtones – *The Isle of Dogs* (1597), co-authored by Thomas Nashe and Ben Jonson; the anonymous *Gowrie*, performed by the King's Men in 1604 – were instantly closed down, and no copy remains of them today.

This urban milieu is increasingly mirrored in the plays of the period. In the late 1590s the 'humours' comedies of Jonson and Chapman anatomised the foibles and follies of the urban middle classes; this spills over, around the turn of the century, into the so-called 'War of the Theatres', in which rival playwrights themselves become the targets. Thus the loquacious and combative Horace in Thomas Dekker's *Satiromastix* (1601) is a thinly disguised caricature of Ben Jonson, with his 'face full of pocky-holes and pimples' like a 'rotten russet apple'. According to contemporary gossip, Shakespeare took part in this satirical war and gave that 'pestilent fellow' Jonson 'a purge which made him bewray his credit': what form this literary laxative took remains uncertain – there may be elements of Jonson in big morose Ajax in *Troilus and Cressida*, performed in about 1602.

Early Jacobean drama has a topical, documentary vein, as distinct from the better-known revenge tragedies of the period. There are 'city comedies' and 'apprentice comedies' with closely realised London settings. There are dramatised versions of real-life murder cases, such as the *Miseries of Enforced Marriage* (c.1607) by the hack author and brothel-keeper George Wilkins, and

View of London from Southwark with the Globe theatre and Bear Garden in the foreground (detail)
Wenceslaus Hollar, c.1670
In Hollar's famous 'Long View' of London, the labels of the Globe theatre and the 'bear baiting house' (also known as the Hope theatre) are reversed. The circular Globe ('this wooden O', as Shakespeare styled it) is seen in a surprisingly leafy setting. Hollar shows the rebuilt Globe: the original one was destroyed by fire in 1613, when a cannonade ignited the thatch during a performance of Shakespeare and Fletcher's *Henry VIII*.

The Roaring Girle.

OR

Moll Cut-Purse.

As it hath lately beene Acted on the Fortune-stage by
the *Prince his Players.*

Written by *T. Middleton* and *T. Dekkar.*

My case is alter'd, I must worke for my living.

Printed at *London* for *Thomas Archer*, and are to be sold at his
shop in Popes head-pallace, neere the Royall.
Exchange. 1611.

the anonymous *Yorkshire Tragedy* (1608), attributed improbably on the title-page to 'W. Shakespeare'. And there is Dekker and Thomas Middleton's *The Roaring Girl* (1611), a lively confection of fact and fantasy, not unlike a Hollywood biopic today, which recounts the exploits of the notorious Mary Frith, alias Moll or Mal Cutpurse. Some performances of this play were enlivened by the presence of Moll herself, who 'sat upon the stage, in the public view of all the people there present, in man's apparel, & played upon her lute and sang a song'.

Perhaps more than the court, the background of Shakespeare the writer is a London street, with its cross-section of citizens, apprentices, servants, criminals, prostitutes and beggars. The inhabitants of Shoreditch, Bishopsgate, Cripplegate and Southwark – all recorded as areas where Shakespeare had lodgings – are transmuted into Falstaff, Pistol, Constable Elbow and Mistress Overdone. The literature of the period opened up to the raw stuff of daily life. You cannot write about a day at the fair, Jonson says in his preface to *Bartholomew Fair* (1614), without a language that 'savours of Smithfield, the booth and the pig-broth'. The pamphleteers made urban low-life one of their stocks in trade – Greene's 'conny-catching' pamphlets detailing the lore and language of the Elizabethan underworld; Dekker's *The Wonderful Year* (1603) with its grim account of the city gripped by bubonic plague. These horrific epidemics decimated whole

....

OPPOSITE

Title page of *The Roaring Girl* by Thomas Middleton and Thomas Dekker
Unknown artist, published 1611
The appearance onstage of the thief Mary or Marian Frith, aka 'Moll Cutpurse', dressed as a man and smoking a pipe, epitomises the Jacobean dramatists' fascination with the London underworld. She may also be the protagonist of a lost jest-book, *The Mad Pranks of Merry Mal of the Bankside* (1610). She served time in both Bridewell and Bedlam, and died in 1659.

neighbourhoods. Nashe gives a figure of 1,800 deaths a week in the hot summer of 1593, and writes an exquisite song in his play *Summer's Last Will* (1600):

> The plague full swift goes by,
> I am sick, I must die.

The court and the city were the twin poles of the author's life, but another possibility, thoroughly congenial in times of plague, was to find some kind of service or employment in a noble household in the country. Writers had an ambivalent status there: they might be tutors or secretaries, or merely time-beguiling conversationalists. Some lived in permanent semi-retirement in country houses, as did the poet Samuel Daniel at Wilton House, near Salisbury, home of the Earls of Pembroke. Others found more temporary refuge – in 1593, after a spell in Newgate prison, Nashe recuperated on the Isle of Wight as the guest of Sir George Carey; around the same time Shakespeare may have stayed at Titchfield with the Earl of Southampton, to whom he dedicated his poems *Venus and Adonis* (1593) and *Lucrece* (1594). The English country house hovers hazily in the background of many great works of the period, such as Sidney's *Arcadia*, written at Wilton in the early 1580s, and Jonson's 'Ode to Penshurst':

> Thou art not, Penshurst, built to envious show
> Of touch or marble, nor canst boast a row
> Of polished pillars or a roof of gold ...
> Thou joy'st in better marks: of soil, of air,
> Of wood, of water – therein thou art fair.

The east front of Wilton House
Wilton House, near Salisbury, was the home of Mary, Countess of Pembroke, the sister
of Sir Philip Sidney. In its day, the house was a seat of learning and poetry, 'like a college'.

Sir Francis Drake
Nicholas Hilliard, 1581
Irascible, courageous and ruthless, Drake is the epitome of the Elizabethan sea dog. The Spanish called him 'the master-thief of the known universe'; the Queen dissociated herself from his piracies but was glad enough of her share of the profits. His body lies in a lead coffin somewhere off the coast of Panama.

These great estates and hunting-parks tend to feature more in the literature than does the rural world beyond the gatehouse. The real countryside is edited out, or repackaged as a pastoral landscape full of piping swains and comic yokels. Shakespeare is an exception, giving us rich glimpses of rural England as it hit the eye –'low farms, poor pelting villages, sheep-cotes and mills'; an oak tree 'with great ragg'd horns'; the 'drowned field' and the 'rooky wood'. A famous line in *Hamlet*, 'There's a divinity that shapes our ends, rough-hew them how we will', borrows terms used by Warwickshire hedgers.

And further, beyond the court and the city and the country house, beyond the narrow horizons of England, there was the wider world, which the three-year circumnavigation by Sir Francis Drake (1578–80) seemed to bring within the reach of every Englishman. The New World of America promised fabulous wealth, but also a fascinating sense of difference, of the exotic, and a hint of a lost age of innocence: 'we found the people most

Theire sitting at meate.

....
**A native American man
and woman eating**
John White, 1585–6
John White was a member
of the Virginia expedition of
1585, and produced a series
of beautiful watercolours
depicting tribal life and customs
among the Algonquin Indians.
His granddaughter, Virginia
Dare, was the first English person
to be born on American soil.

gentle, loving and faithful,' wrote Arthur Barlowe from Virginia
in 1584, 'and such as live after the manner of the Golden Age'.
This new landscape of boundless possibilities is also found in
the literature of the day, from Othello's 'anthropophagai, and
men whose heads do grow beneath their shoulders', to John
Donne's ironic 'discovering' – i.e. undressing – of his mistress:
'O my America! My New-found-land!'

In the biographical sketches that follow there is a mix of
documentary and anecdotal evidence. Much of the latter comes
from the great seventeenth-century memoirists – John Aubrey,
Thomas Fuller, Sir Robert Naunton, Izaak Walton. They were
excellent historians, but also avid jotters-down of ephemera
and gossip; their stories are irresistible but usually unverifiable.
Nonetheless, they were a lot closer to the Elizabethans than
we are, and their sources were in some cases eyewitnesses.

There are also elements of factual uncertainty in the portraits
assembled here. Some are conjecturally identified; some are later

copies of lost originals. In many cases the artists are anonymous. Few writers were of sufficient status to warrant a portrait by the famous artists of the period: we have a pair of superb miniatures by Nicholas Hilliard, but their subjects (Mary Sidney and Sir Walter Ralegh) were not being painted *because* they were writers. The painters of the day were in some measure analagous to the professional writers: brilliant craftsmen who made a precarious living out of what we would now call 'art' but which was then generally thought of as a skilled trade. Many were of immigrant stock – Isaac Oliver, Johann de Critz, Hieronimo Custodis, Marcus Gheeraerts – bringing other influences, other landscapes, into the rich melting-pot of Elizabethan and Jacobean England.

Questions and uncertainties remain, but at least these pictures have survived. So much from the period is lost. Writers of the stature of John Lyly, Thomas Kyd, John Marston, Thomas Dekker and John Webster are missing from this gallery. No portrait of them survives; they are faceless. So one is grateful to the often unknown painters, engravers and draughtsmen whose works are reproduced here, and to the known ones such as Martin Droeshout, whose unlovely picture of Shakespeare may not be as good or beautiful as the book it illustrates, but is in some ways as precious.

....
OPPOSITE
Isaac Oliver
Self-portrait, c.1590
The French Huguenot immigrant Isaac Oliver trained as a 'limner' or miniature-painter under Nicholas Hilliard, and married the sister of another immigrant painter, Marcus Gheeraerts the Younger. This vibrant self-portrait, 51mm across, was once owned by the eighteenth-century collector Horace Walpole, who found its 'imitation of nature' so fine 'that the largest magnifying glass only calls out new beauties'.

BIOGRAPHIES

William Shakespeare (1564–1616)

Universally considered the greatest of Elizabethan writers – 'the soul of the age,' as Ben Jonson put it – Shakespeare remains a somewhat shadowy figure. Though famous in his day, he did not attract personal publicity in the way that Marlowe and Jonson did, nor did he pursue courtly preferment. The acquisition of a family coat of arms – motto 'Non sans droit' (not without right) parodied by Jonson as 'Not without mustard' – and the steady accumulation of property are the documented signs of his success.

'He was not a company-keeper,' says John Aubrey, and 'wouldn't be debauched'. He devoted his life to the theatre, as an actor and company-shareholder as well as a writer. His collected works, Mr William Shakespeare's Comedies, Histories, and Tragedies, better known as the First Folio of 1623, contains thirty-six plays. A later edition (1664) added Pericles to the canon, and there are other, earlier works, such as Edward III, now thought to be his.

Born in Stratford, the son of a glover, Shakespeare was brought up in what may have been a discreetly Catholic family. In 1582, at the age of eighteen, he married a local woman, Anne Hathwey or Hathaway, by whom he had three children: Susanna, conceived out of wedlock and born in 1583, and the twins Hamnet and Judith, born in 1585. Hamnet died at the age of eleven. Shakespeare's whereabouts during most of the 1580s are unknown. It has been argued that he was in Lancashire, serving in Catholic households, and that he is the William 'Shakeshafte' who is mentioned in Alexander Hoghton's will of 1581 and who

....
OPPOSITE
William Shakespeare
associated with John Taylor, c.1610
The so-called 'Chandos' portrait, named after one of its owners.

probably served as one of Sir Thomas Hesketh's players at Rufford Hall thereafter. However, Aubrey says that 'he had been in his younger years a schoolmaster in the country', and Edmond Malone thought that he had been a lawyer's clerk.

He is certainly the 'Shake-scene' attacked by the popular author Robert Greene in 1592, by which time he had achieved prominence, in London, as an actor and author. Greene writes:

> There is an upstart crow beautified with our feathers, that with his 'Tiger's heart wrapped in a player's hide' supposes he is as well able to bombast out a blank verse as the best of you; and being an absolute Johannes Factotum [jack of all trades] is in his own conceit the only Shake-scene in a country. (*Greene's Groatsworth of Wit*, 1592)

The line about the 'Tiger's heart' parodies a line from Shakespeare's *Henry VI Part 3*, 'O tiger's heart wrapped in a woman's hide'. A few months later, the author Henry Chettle, who had edited *Greene's Groatsworth* after the latter's death, made some amends for this, saying:

> Myself have seen his demeanour no less civil than he excellent in the quality he professes. Besides, divers of worship have reported his uprightness of dealing, which argues his honesty, and his facetious grace in writing, which approves his art. (*Kind-Heart's Dream*, 1592)

Shakespeare's first published works were poems rather than plays – *Venus and Adonis* (1593) and *Lucrece* (1594), both dedicated to Henry Wriothesley, 3rd Earl of Southampton. The latter is also

....
A scene from *Titus Andronicus*

Henry Peacham, 1594

This drawing by Henry Peacham, author of *The Compleat Gentleman* (1622), is our only contemporary visual record of a Shakespeare production. It illustrates a scene from the early and gruesome tragedy *Titus Andronicus* (1594), where Queen Tamora pleads for the life of her sons Alarbus and Demetrius. One notes the costumes – an ad hoc mixture of Classical and Elizabethan – and the lively figure of the scheming 'blackamoor' Aaron.

thought to be the 'Fair Youth' addressed in the *Sonnets*, though the identity of the antithetical 'Dark Lady' is still debated. From 1594, Shakespeare was an actor and shareholder in the Lord Chamberlain's Men; the pre-eminence of this troupe was formally recognised in 1603, when they became the King's Men. Revels accounts record the performance of plays by 'Shaxberd' at court, but the company's theatrical residence was the Globe, built in 1599 with the dismantled timbers of the Theatre in Shoreditch. Later they performed at the private theatre in Blackfriars owned by the actor Richard Burbage; for this more intimate setting his last plays were written. *The Tempest* (c.1611) has the air of a farewell –

> Our revels now are ended. These our actors,
> As I foretold you, were all spirits, and
> Are melted into air, into thin air … .

But Shakespeare later collaborated with John Fletcher on *Henry VIII* (c.1613), and probably also on the lost *Cardenio* (c.1613) and *The Two Noble Kinsmen* (c.1614).

Aubrey describes him as 'a handsome, well-shaped man, very good company, and of a very ready and pleasant smooth wit'. The best-known image of him is the Folio engraving by Martin Droeshout (see page 4). It was probably based on a lost picture: the stiff, wired collar suggests a date of c.1604 or later for the original, when Shakespeare was in his forties. It is not known which of the two immigrant artists named Martin Droeshout (uncle and nephew) engraved the portrait.

Much more atmospheric is the 'Chandos' portrait (page 39). The features are similar to those of the Droeshout, but the painting is full of drama – the dark, almost Latin cast, the

....
Drawing of the Swan theatre, London
Arendt van Buchell after Johannes
De Witt's sketch of 1596
While we have only exterior views
of the Globe, this sketch gives a
groundling's eye-view of the interior
of the neighbouring Swan theatre
shortly after its opening in 1595.
We see a deep projecting stage,
three tiers of galleries, two stage
entrances, and the dressing-room
(*mimorum aedes*) with a balcony above
containing the 'lords' rooms' or boxes.
An accompanying note states that the
galleries alone accommodated up to
3,000 spectators.

piratical earring, the guarded gaze. Though its identity as a
portrait of Shakespeare remains unproven, it has a documentary
pedigree that takes us almost back to the painting of it. It takes its
name from the Chandos family and was catalogued among their
collection at Stowe in 1747. Its earlier provenance is summed up
in an intriguing note by the eighteenth-century engraver and
art historian George Vertue:

> The picture of Shakespeare. Original of Mr Keyck of the
> Temple. He bought [it] for forty guineas of Mr Baterton,
> who bought of Sr W Davenant, to whom it was left by will
> of John Taylor … . It was painted by Taylor, a player & painter
> contemp with Shakes & his intimate friend. (*Notebooks*, I)

Assiduous detective work has fleshed out much of this history
of ownership, taking us back in time from the barrister Robert

Keck, who owned it in 1719, to the actor Thomas Betterton, and thence to Sir William Davenant, the seventeenth-century poet and playwright who claimed to be Shakespeare's godson and/or illegitimate child. The identification of the artist himself remains complex. Attention has focused on a John Taylor who was a young actor with the Paul's Boys in 1598; and a John Taylor who was a member of the Company of Painter-Stainers by 1626, and who died in 1651. Might these perhaps be the same John Taylor, and might he be the artist described by Vertue as both 'player & painter'? It is possible. One cannot be certain, as so often with the Elizabethans, and indeed the eyes that look out somewhat warily from the picture do not suggest much faith in certainties.

His last years – he probably retired to Stratford around 1613 – have a crabby, local-landowner tone: there are lawsuits and accusations of 'engrossing', or stockpiling, grain in times of need. According to tradition, Shakespeare died at his home, New Place, after overindulging in the company of Jonson and Michael Drayton: 'Drayton and Ben Jonson had a merry meeting, and, it seems, drank too hard, for Shakespeare died of a fever there contracted' (Revd John Ward, Vicar of Stratford, c.1662). The somewhat abstemious tenor of his life tends to argue against this; a more recent conjecture, based on mortality records in the area, suggests he may have succumbed to typhoid fever. The limestone bust of Shakespeare incorporated into his monument in Holy Trinity Church in Stratford was in situ by 1623 (it is referred to by Leonard Digges in prefatory verses in the First Folio). Its sculptor was probably Gheerart Janssen (or Gerard Johnson) the Younger. It is the least attractive of the images of Shakespeare – plump and bourgeois – but this may indeed be much how Shakespeare looked in his last years.

....

William Shakespeare
Plaster cast after Gerard Johnson's marble effigy at Stratford-upon-Avon, c.1620

Christopher Marlowe (1564–93)

Kit Marlowe was the wild boy of Elizabethan literature, the wayward young genius cut short in his prime. He was twenty-nine years old when he died in a knife fight at Deptford, on the outskirts of London. During his brief life, Marlowe was both revered and reviled: 'Wit sent from heaven but vices sent from hell'. His 'wit' survives in half a dozen plays, including that great Elizabethan spine-chiller Dr Faustus, and some fine lyric poetry. His 'vices' were (or were said to be) atheism, blasphemy and homosexuality – not just vices, at this time, but crimes.

Born in Canterbury, the son of a shoemaker, he was an exact contemporary of Shakespeare. They later knew one another; during his lifetime Marlowe was the more famous. At sixteen he won a scholarship to Cambridge, but his career there was chequered. In 1587 the authorities accused him of subversive Catholic activities and refused to grant his degree, but the Privy Council dispatched an exonerating letter saying Marlowe 'had done her Majesty good service' in certain confidential 'affairs'. The kind of service is not specified, but the context suggests anti-Catholic espionage. Marlowe's college accounts are extant and show an unexpected flush of spending money in 1585–6.

His earliest theatrical success was Tamburlaine the Great, performed in 1587. He hastily cobbled up a sequel; at a performance of the latter, by the Admiral's Men, an accidentally loaded gun went off on stage, killing two of the spectators. Only five other plays are known: Dido, Dr Faustus, The Jew of Malta, Massacre at Paris and Edward II. This is the probable order of their composition, but no fixed dates are known. The plays are full of passionate poetry – his 'high astounding terms', as he put it – but their undertone

....

Unknown man called Christopher Marlowe

Unknown artist, 1585

The history of this painting is unknown prior to 1953, when it was discovered in a pile of builder's rubble in Cambridge. It has been proposed as Marlowe because his dates fit with the inscription and because it turned up at Corpus Christi College, where he was a student in 1585. Add to this a sense of aptness: the sardonic gaze, the snazzy jacket, the troubling motto QUOD ME NUTRIT ME DESTRUIT – 'What feeds me destroys me'. Possibly the portrait relates to that spell of government 'service' cited by the Privy Council. The young man does not look like a Cambridge scholar, but he may look like an ambitious young player in the dangerous waters of Elizabethan politics.

of irony and black humour, and their rapidity of action, make them very modern. T.S. Eliot said that Marlowe's tragedies were something more like 'serious, even savage' farce.

Much that we know of his adult life is in police records. In 1589 he was imprisoned after a street-fight in which an innkeeper's son was killed (though not by him). In 1592 he was arrested in the Netherlands on a charge of 'coining', or counterfeiting money, and was deported to be examined by Lord Burghley. He was also accused of 'intent to go to the enemy', in other words, of defecting to the Spanish Catholic forces. This is probably another episode in Marlowe's shadowy career as a spy. In the same year he was in trouble for 'disturbing the peace' in Shoreditch and, on a visit to Canterbury, for menacing a tailor named Corkine with 'a dagger and a staff'.

Among his friends were the poets Thomas Watson and George Chapman, the pamphleteer Thomas Nashe and the scientist Thomas Harriot; and his patrons were intellectual noblemen such as Lord Strange and the Earl of Northumberland. Another patron was Thomas Walsingham, a young cousin of the spymaster Sir Francis.

Marlowe's connection with the freethinking clique of Northumberland and Ralegh brought him into political danger. It was said he 'had read the atheist lecture' to them, and had circulated a 'book against the Trinity'. In May 1593 a series of charges were laid against him by the spy Richard Baines, who had been the cause of his arrest in the Netherlands. The 'Baines Note' is a terrific itemisation of Marlowe's 'damnable opinions' and heresies, among them:

Sir Francis Walsingham
attributed to John de
Critz the Elder, c.1585
As Secretary of State,
Walsingham ran what
is generally credited as
the first 'secret service'
in English history, and
Marlowe was just one
of many young men
caught up in the web of
Elizabethan espionage.
De Critz's portrait of
'Mr Secretary' conveys his
Machiavellian political
cunning – he was a
'most subtle searcher of
hidden secrets' (William
Camden) – while the
sombre garb and the
skull-cap suggest his
Puritan leanings.

... That Moses was but a juggler
... That the first beginning of religion was only to keep
men in awe
... That Christ was a bastard and his mother dishonest
... That St John the Evangelist was bedfellow to Christ,
and leaned always in his bosom, and that he used him
as the sinners of Sodoma
... That all they that love not tobacco & boys were fools

Further information was extracted from his former chamber-
fellow Thomas Kyd. It was Marlowe's 'custom', he affirmed,
'to jest at the divine scriptures, jibe at prayers'. Some of Kyd's

comments on Marlowe suggest a genuine recoiling: 'he was intemperate & of a cruel heart,' Kyd said.

On 20 May 1593 Marlowe was examined before the Privy Council, but he remained at liberty, on bail. Ten days later, he met up with three men at a riverside lodging house in Deptford. They were spies and fraudsters, his colleagues in the underworld. He died that evening, stabbed through the right eye by one of his companions, Ingram Frizer. According to the coroner's inquest, they had quarrelled over the 'reckoning', or bill, for the day's food and drink. Frizer was acquitted on a plea of self-defence, but questions remain about the killing.

Poets mourned the loss of 'the Muses' darling' (George Peele); of 'neat Marlowe' – neat in the sense of unadulterated – 'whose raptures were all air and fire' (Michael Drayton). But to the Puritans, his violent end was a 'manifest sign of God's judgement' upon him. 'See what a hook the Lord put in the nostrils of this barking dog,' thundered the preacher Thomas Beard (who was many years later Oliver Cromwell's schoolteacher).

Shakespeare quotes from Marlowe in *As You Like It* (c.1599) and calls him the 'dead shepherd', and an enigmatic line spoken by Touchstone, the play's clown, seems to comment on the circumstances of Marlowe's death: 'It strikes a man more dead than a great reckoning in a little room.'

Ben Jonson (1572–1637)

Ben Jonson was the comic genius of the age. His career as dramatist, masque-writer and poet spanned four decades and three reigns, and produced nearly forty plays. He was a big-gestured, quarrelsome, heavy-drinking man:

> He would many times exceed in drink (Canary was his beloved liquor), then he would tumble home to bed, and when he had thoroughly perspired, then to study. I have seen his studying chair, which was of straw, such as old women used. (John Aubrey, *Brief Lives*, MS, late seventeenth century)

Yet his writing is more punctiliously 'classical' than that of any of his contemporaries. John Dryden singled him out as 'the greatest man of the last age', but found in him something difficult and off-putting, adding, 'I admire him, but I love Shakespeare.'

According to his own account, Jonson was the son of a Protestant minister, from a Scottish family which forfeited its estates during the reign of Mary Tudor. He was 'posthumous born' a month after the death of his father. His mother married a bricklayer, Robert Brett. He was 'brought up poorly', on Harts Horn Lane near Charing Cross, but was able to study at Westminster School under the great William Camden. In his youth Jonson was variously an apprentice bricklayer, a soldier in the Low Countries and a strolling actor. At the age of twenty-one he married Anne Lewis: she bore him four children, three of whom died young. His poem on the death of his infant daughter Mary ends:

This grave partakes the fleshly birth,
Which cover lightly, gentle earth.

In 1597 Jonson was imprisoned for his part in writing a
'lewd, slanderous and seditious' play, The Isle of Dogs, part-written
by Thomas Nashe; and again the following year, after killing the
actor Gabriel Spenser in a sword fight.

With Every Man in His Humour (1598), performed by the Lord
Chamberlain's Men with Shakespeare in the cast, Jonson began a
long run of successful, brilliantly crafted, topical comedies, including
Volpone (1605), The Alchemist (1610) and Bartholomew Fair (1614).
Around the turn of the century he was involved in the public mud-
slinging of the 'War of the Theatres' and traded insults with rival
playwrights. Thomas Dekker said that Jonson's face was like a
'rotten russet apple when 'tis bruised' and his voice 'sounds so i'
th' nose'. At gentlemen's tables he would 'fling epigrams, emblems
and play-speeches about him like hail-stones' (Satiromastix, 1601).

In 1605 Jonson was peripherally involved in the government's
investigation of the Gunpowder Plot. He espoused Catholicism for
some years, then in about 1610 returned to the Protestant fold: 'At
his first communion, in token of true reconciliation, he drank out
all the full cup of wine' (William Drummond). In 1619 he walked
from London to Scotland – the journey took him about ten weeks;
he bought a new pair of shoes in Darlington. At Hawthornden
Castle, near Edinburgh, he stayed with the poet William
Drummond, who left this sketch of him:

....
OPPOSITE
Ben Jonson
Abraham van Blyenberch, c.1617
Van Blyenberch's vigorous brushstrokes seem to capture something of Johnson's colourful
character. All other known portraits of the playwright appear to derive from this one.

He is a great lover and praiser of himself, a contemner and scorner of others, given rather to lose a friend than a jest, jealous of every word and action of those about him (especially after drink, which is one of the elements in which he liveth), a dissembler of ill parts which reign in him, a bragger of some good that he wanteth, thinketh nothing well but what either he himself or some of his friends and countrymen hath said or done. He is passionately kind and angry, careless either to gain or keep, vindictive, but if he be well answered, at himself.

In his youth Jonson was thin – 'a hollow-cheekt scrag', Dekker calls him – but by the time of his Scottish expedition he was a twenty-stone giant: he speaks of 'my mountain belly, my rocky face'.

A portrait of Jonson by the Dutch artist Abraham van Blyenberch is mentioned in an inventory of the Duke of Buckingham's pictures in 1635, two years before Jonson's death. This is probably the portrait in the National Portrait Gallery illustrated here (see page 52). Blyenberch was working in England between 1617 and 1620, so in this image we probably see Jonson in his mid-forties. There is a glisten on his skin that one might relate to his fondness for Canary wine, and a suggestion of those facial blemishes mentioned by Dekker. In the engraving by Robert Vaughan, from the mid-1620s, the great comic writer has a dour, haggard look – comedy, he seems to say, is no longer a laughing matter. This engraving bears out Aubrey's comment that 'Ben Jonson had one eye lower than t'other and bigger', but equally it may be the source of Aubrey's description. Both images convey the power of Jonson's personality. It was one

of his sayings that 'he would not flatter, though he saw
death', and his look seems to challenge the artists not to
flatter him either.

Bedridden from a stroke, Jonson lived his last years at
the Gate House at Westminster, with a drunken housekeeper
and a pet fox. His epitaph in Poets' Corner reads simply:
'O Rare Ben Jonson'.

John Fletcher
Unknown artist, late seventeenth century, after an original of c.1620
The portrait of Fletcher in the collection of the Earl of Clarendon (of which the portrait illustrated here is a later version) shows him with light brown hair and a wispy beard, in costume suggesting a date of c.1620. He would then have been in his early forties.

Francis Beaumont (1584–1616) and John Fletcher (1579–1625)

Beaumont and Fletcher wrote a dozen plays together in the early years of the seventeenth century, among them *The Knight of the Burning Pestle* (c.1607), *Philaster* (1609) and *The Maid's Tragedy* (1610–11). Though both wrote solo works, they are best known as collaborators:

> John Fletcher and Francis Beaumont esquire, like Castor and Pollux (most happy when in conjunction), raised the English to equal the Athenian and Roman theatre; Beaumont bringing the ballast of judgement, Fletcher the sail of fantasy, both compounding a poet to admiration. (Thomas Fuller, *Worthies of England*, 1660)

Beaumont was the youngest son of a well-to-do Leicestershire magistrate. He left Oxford without taking a degree and in 1600 came to London, where he enrolled at the fashionable Inner Temple. He was part of Ben Jonson's circle, and was one of the famous company of wits who met at the Mermaid tavern in Bread Street. His earliest play, *The Woman Hater* (c.1605), is a Jonsonian 'comedy of humours'. His friendship with Fletcher dates from around this time:

> They lived together on the Bankside, not far from the playhouse [the Globe], both bachelors; lay together; had one wench in the house between them, which they did so admire; the same clothes etc. between them. (John Aubrey, *Brief Lives*)

Iudicis argutum que negl   *Formidat.*   *Touperit Hos.*

FRANCIS
BEAVMONT. Esq

Ob. A° Ætat. Circt XXC AD.1615.

Geo. Vertue Sculp. 1729.

Celsissimo Principi LEONELLO Duci de DORSET &c.
Nobilissimo Ordinis Periscelides Equiti.
Hanc Tabulam ad Archetypum in ipsius Ædibus expressam Humil. D.D.D. G. Vertue

Beaumont married advantageously and retired from London to Kent in c.1612. The countryside did not suit him: 'the little wit I had is lost,' he complains. The days of wine and repartee at the Mermaid seemed suddenly distant:

... What things have we seen,
Done at the Mermaid? Heard words that have been
So nimble and so full of subtle flame
As if that everyone from whom they came
Had meant to put his whole wit in a jest,
And had resolved to live a fool the rest
Of his dull life ... .
(Verse-letter to Ben Jonson, c.1612)

After Beaumont's death, Ben Jonson sourly remarked to William Drummond, 'Beaumont loved too much himself and his own verses.'

John Fletcher was from a family of preachers and writers. His father, Richard Fletcher, was chaplain at the execution of Mary Stuart in 1587 and later became Bishop of London; his uncle Giles Fletcher was a scholar and diplomat, and wrote a celebrated book about Russia (*Of the Russe Commonwealth*, 1591); his cousins Phineas and Giles junior were both poets. Fletcher himself studied at Corpus Christi College, Cambridge (Marlowe's former

....
OPPOSITE
Francis Beaumont
George Vertue, 1729
There is a portrait of Beaumont at Knole, Kent, dating from 1615, which shows a handsome, strong face, expressive hands and the twirled moustachios and square-cut beard that are his trademark features in later engravings, such as the early eighteenth-century one by George Vertue illustrated here.

college), but his studies were curtailed when his father died in debt in 1596. His huge output of plays – in all he wrote or co-wrote over fifty – was doubtless dictated by financial need. His collaboration with Shakespeare, at the end of the latter's career, is a mark of respect from the older author.

From two former actors, John Lowin and Joseph Taylor, we get a glimpse of Fletcher mingling with the audience at one of his plays. 'We have known him unconcerned, and to have wished it had been none of his,' but if the play went down well 'he, as well as the thronged theatre (in despite of his innate modesty), applauding this rare issue of his brain'.

Fletcher died in Southwark. According to Aubrey, 'Invited to go with a knight into Norfolk or Suffolk in the plague time, 1625, [he] stayed but to make himself a suit of clothes, and while it was making, fell sick of the plague and died.' He was buried at St Saviour's, now Southwark Cathedral. The playwright Philip Massinger, his close friend, is said to have been buried 'in the same grave' when he died in 1640.

Actors

Both Shakespeare and Jonson began their careers as
'players', but the theatrical boom of the early 1590s soon
produced a generation of actors who might be called the
superstars of the day.

The first to achieve this status was **Edward Alleyn**
(1566–1626), a London innkeeper's son, born in the district
outside Bishopsgate where the earliest theatres were built. The
spelling 'Alleyn' is consistently used, though to the pamphleteer
Nashe, who gives us our first notice of him, he was simply 'Ned
Allen'. Alleyn was famously associated with Marlowe's tragic
heroes, most of them more villain than hero. He performed
the title roles in *Tamburlaine*, *Dr Faustus* and *The Jew of Malta*, and
probably played the Duke of Guise in *Massacre at Paris*. 'He made
any part, especially a majestick one, to become him,' said Bishop
Fuller. In 1592 he married the stepdaughter of Philip Henslowe,
proprietor of the Rose theatre. Alleyn made a great deal of money
and, like Shakespeare, he ploughed it into property, creating
a respectability which his profession did not itself command.
Large profits from bear-baiting – he was part-owner of the
Paris Gardens baiting house – formed part of his wealth.

The great theatrical dynasty of the period was the Burbage
family. In the 1570s James Burbage, an actor in the Earl of
Leicester's troupe, built the first public theatre in London, simply
known as the Theatre. His son **Richard Burbage** (1568–1619), the
legendary interpreter of Shakespearian roles, first trod the boards
as Hamlet, Lear and Othello. While Alleyn was in an earlier, more
stentorian mould, Burbage was a performer of great sublety and
psychological specificity. As Hamlet he delivered to the Players

those marvellous Shakespearian tips on acting, and one assumes his own style accorded with the advice:

> Speak the speech, I pray you, as I pronounced it you, trippingly on the tongue ... Nor do not saw the air too much with your hand, thus, but use all gently, for in the very torrent, tempest and, I may say, whirlwind of your passion, you must acquire and beget a temperance that may give it smoothness.

Written in about 1600, Hamlet also comments topically on the rise of the boys' companies: 'an eyrie of children' or 'little eyasses' (an 'eyass' is a fledgling hawk, but it is hard to resist hearing an indecorous pun) who 'are now the fashion, and so berattle the common stages'. These highly trained young ensembles – chief among them the Children of the Chapel Royal and the Children of St Paul's – offered an elegant alternative to the 'robustious' (Hamlet's word) fare of the public theatres. At this time the rising star of the boys' companies was thirteen-year-old **Nathaniel Field** (1587–1633), who performed in Jonson's *Cynthia's Revels* (1601); he is probably the 'Ned Field' whom Jonson calls his 'scholar'. Field pursued his career into adulthood – he is among the 'principal actors' of Shakespeare's plays listed in the First Folio – and he wrote some minor but charming plays, such as *A Woman is a Weathercock* (1612).

....

OPPOSITE

Edward Alleyn

British School, 1626

In 1613 Alleyn founded the chapel and college at Dulwich, and this dignified, prosperous looking portrait of him hangs there still. His voluminous papers and diaries are also at Dulwich, though unfortunately a few are marred with addenda by the Victorian forger John Payne Collier.

Richard Burbage
British School
According to a contemporary jest, when he was playing Richard III Burbage had
an assignation with a female admirer, but on arriving found Shakespeare being
'intertained' in his stead; the latter sent him word 'that William the Conqueror
was before Richard the Third' (Diary of John Manningham, 13 March 1602).

NATHANIEL FIELD
a Celebrated Actor in Shakespeare Plays .
for the List of Actors in the Best Folio Edition.
from an Original Picture in Dulwich College.

Nathan Field
William Nelson Gardiner
after Sylvester Harding after an
unknown artist, published 1790

No troupe was complete without its star comedian.
The earliest of the great Elizabethan stage clowns was **Richard
Tarlton** (d.1588) – indeed the theatrical sense of 'clown', which
hitherto merely meant a yokel, seems to have originated with
him. He was the Queen's Men's comic in the 1580s, and played
Derrick in the pre-Shakespearian *Henry V*. Stow praised his
'wondrous, plentiful, pleasant, extemporal wit' and Nashe
records the audience's instant laughter 'when Tarlton first peept
out his head'. He died on Holywell Street, now Shoreditch High
Street, in the house of a prostitute named Em Ball.

Two comedians are associated with Shakespeare and a kind
of watershed between them is discernible in his comedies around
the turn of the century. **Will Kempe** (fl.1586–1603) – an old-style
'jigs and bawdry' comic – was undoubtedly the creator of rustic
boobies like Dogberry in *Much Ado About Nothing*. When he left the
Chamberlain's Men in about 1599, perhaps unwillingly, his place

....
Richard Tarlton
Sylvester Harding after an
unknown artist, published 1792

....
Will Kempe
Will Kempe, 1600
Engraving after a woodcut on
the title page of Kempe's *Nine
Days Wonder*

was filled by **Robert Armin** (c.1575–1615), who played the more
melancholy, wry 'fools', such as Feste in *Twelfth Night* and the Fool
in *King Lear*. Something of Kempe's style is caught in his memoir,
Kempe's Nine Days Wonder (1600), which recounts his feat, or stunt,
of morris dancing from London to Norwich. Armin was also an
author, though such works as *A Nest of Ninnies* (1608) convey little
of the inferred subtlety of his theatrical performances.

THE

History of the two Maids of More-clacke,

VVith the life and simple maner of IOHN
in the Hospitall.

Played by the Children of the Kings
Maiesties Reuels.

VVritten by ROBERT ARMIN, seruant to the Kings
most excellent Maiestie.

LONDON,
Printed by *N.O.* for *Thomas Archer,* and is to be sold at his
shop in Popes head Pallace, 1 6 0 9.

ROBERT ARMIN.
was an Actor in Shakspears Plays.
See the list of Actors in the first Folio Edition.
London Pub Aprill.1.1790. by E.Harding N.º.132 Fleet Street.

....
Robert Armin
after an unknown artist, 1790;
first published 1609

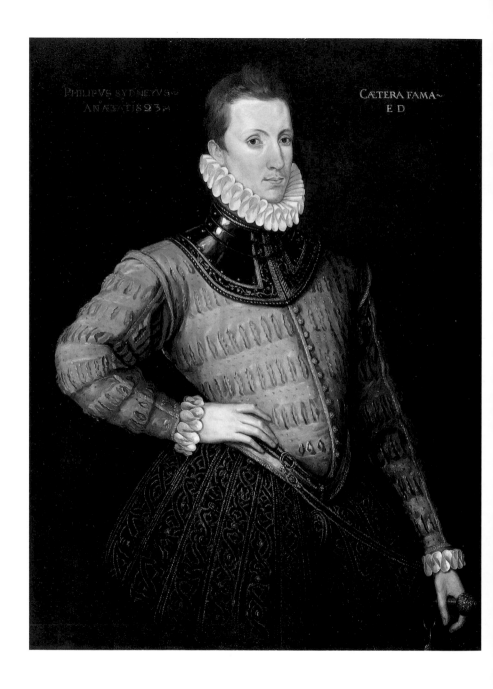

The Sidney Circle

Attractive, talented and well connected, **Sir Philip Sidney** (1554–86) and his sister **Mary Herbert, Countess of Pembroke** (1561–1621), were figureheads – Philip as poet, Mary as patron – of a certain kind of Elizabethan writing: refined, pastoral, philosophical, a world away from the rougher, more commercial milieu of playwrights and pamphleteers.

The nephew of the Earl of Leicester, Sidney was 'the most accomplished cavalier of his time'. He was regarded as the Elizabethan ideal of the soldier-poet, the man of action and refinement: 'Mars and Mercury fell at variance whose servant he should be.'

> He was so highly prized in the esteem of the Queen that she thought the court deficient without him … He was a noble and matchless gentleman, and it may be justly said of him that he seemed to be born only to that which he went about: *Versatilis ingenii* [many sided in his genius], as Plutarch hath it. (Sir Robert Naunton, *Fragmenta Regalia*, 1633)

Sidney's fine sonnet sequence *Astrophil and Stella* describes his illicit passion for the Earl of Essex's sister, Penelope Rich, and offers advice pertinent to all writers: '"Fool," said my Muse to me, "look in thy heart and write."' The *Arcadia*, his long philosophical romance, initiated a fashion for the pastoral and his *Defence of Poetry* responded eloquently to Puritan anti-literary diatribes.

....

OPPOSITE
Sir Philip Sidney
Unknown artist, after 1576

....
**Probably Mary Herbert,
Countess of Pembroke**
Nicholas Hilliard, c.1590

Fighting the Spanish in the Netherlands, Sidney was wounded in action at Zutphen – reputedly giving his water bottle to another soldier, saying, 'Thy necessity is yet greater than mine' – and died a month later at Arnheim, aged thirty-two.

The poet Matthew Roydon, who knew Sidney, spoke of his 'sweet attractive kind of grace' (*A Friend's Passion*, c.1586), but Ben Jonson, who is unlikely to have known him, said, 'Sir P Sidney was no pleasant man in countenance, his face being spoiled by pimples, and of high blood, and long' (*Conversations with Drummond*, 1619).

Despite his short life, a number of portraits of Sidney survive. The portrait here is probably an early copy of one at Longleat House, Wiltshire. It shows him at the age of twenty-two, in martial guise, with a decorated steel gorget (or armoured neckpiece) below his ruff. The hair colour just about corresponds with Aubrey's description of it as 'a dark amber'. The portrait originally belonged to Sir William Russell, Sidney's friend, who was with him in the fatal engagement at Zutphen.

Mary Sidney was married at sixteen to Henry Herbert, 2nd Earl of Pembroke, who was nearly thirty years her senior.

'Fair and witty', she became 'the greatest patroness of wit and learning of any lady in her time' (John Aubrey, *Brief Lives*). Her country seat, Wilton House (see page 31), 'was like a college'. Among her protégés were the poets Samuel Daniel and Nicholas Breton, but the Grub-streeter Nashe, who had edited an unauthorised edition of *Astrophil and Stella*, was sent packing. She jealously guarded the memory and literary effects of her brother, and oversaw the definitive edition of the *Arcadia* (1593), much of which had been written in her company at Wilton.

Mary's elder son, William Herbert, later 3rd Earl, was also a patron of poets, but was not the 'Mr W.H.' described as the 'only begetter' of Shakespeare's *Sonnets*. Another son was named after her brother: it was scurrilously said he was Sidney's son, though 'he inherited not the wit of either brother or sister'.

'She had a pretty, sharp, oval face,' says Aubrey, and hair 'of a reddish yellow'. The miniature by Nicholas Hilliard shows her *c.*1590, in her late twenties. The portrait is only a couple of inches wide, and is backed with a snippet of playing-card (a Two of Spades). She aged quickly, if the formidable old dowager engraved by Simon van de Passe in 1618 is an accurate likeness.

Others of the clan had poetic blood in their veins. **Sir Robert Sidney** (1563–1626) grew up in his older brother's shadow, and inherited from him the thankless post of Governor of Flushing (or Vliessingen) in the Netherlands; there, in 1592, he arrested and deported Christopher Marlowe (or 'Marly', as he spells it) on a charge of counterfeiting. He prospered under James, who thought him 'so rare a gentleman', and in 1618 was created Earl of Leicester (being judged the nearest legitimate descendant of the previous Earl, his uncle). His poetry is undistinguished but in one sense unique: his own notebook, containing over sixty

INVENIAM VIAM
AVT FACIAM

ABOVE

Robert Sidney, 1st Earl of Leicester
Unknown artist, c.1588
The baton in Sidney's right hand probably
signifies the Governorship of Flushing,
which he was granted in 1588. The impresa
shows flames bursting through green branches,
with the motto INVENIAM VIAM AUT FACIAM,
signifying that he will 'either find a way or
make one' – a powerful motto of ambition.

OPPOSITE

Mary Wroth, Lady Sidney
attributed to Marcus Gheeraerts
the Younger, c.1620
This vivid full-length portrait shows
Lady Mary Wroth with an archlute.
Ben Jonson mentions the musical
soirées at Durrants, her country-house
in Enfield, where 'Apollo's harp and
Hermes' lyre resound'.

poems, is the longest autograph manuscript by an Elizabethan poet to survive; some of the pages are dense with revision. This notebook, a small quarto bound in green morocco leather, surfaced in the early 1970s and is now in the British Library.

Sir Robert's eldest daughter, **Lady Mary Wroth** (c.1587–c.1651), was also a poet. Before her marriage to Sir Robert Wroth she scandalised polite society by having an affair with her cousin William Herbert, by whom she had two illegitimate children. On Twelfth Night 1605, she performed in Jonson's *Masque of Blackness*, blacked up as an 'Ethiopian nymph', and three years later she reprised the role in Jonson's *Masque of Beauty*. These were somewhat salacious performances: 'Their apparel was rich, but too light and curtizan-like for such great ones' (Dudley Carleton to Sir Ralph Winwood, January 1605). Jonson was a great admirer – he dedicated *The Alchemist* (1610) to her and wrote epigrams in her praise. Her best-known work is her romance *The Countess of Mountgomery's Urania* (1621), published in a handsome folio edition with an engraved frontispiece by van de Passe. The title is a compliment to her friend Susanna, wife of her cousin Philip Herbert, Earl of Montgomery, and an echo of *The Countess of Pembroke's Arcadia* by her uncle, which her book closely imitates. Some took it as a satirical *roman à clef*. Lord Denny was said to be outraged,

> for that in her book of *Urania* she doth palpably and grossly play upon him and his late daughter, the Lady Mary Hay, besides many others she makes bold with; and, they say, takes great liberty, or rather licence, to traduce whom she pleases, and thinks she dances in a net. (John Chamberlain to Dudley Carleton, 9 March 1623)

....
Fulke Greville, 1st Baron Brooke
Joseph John Jenkins, published 1825

Another poetess of the family was Sir Philip's only child, Elizabeth, Countess of Rutland, whom Ben Jonson flatteringly considered 'nothing inferior to her father in poesy'. Drummond records that her fondness for Jonson was not shared by her husband: 'Ben one day being at table with my lady Rutland, her husband coming in accused her that she kept table to poets.'

The web of Philip Sidney's literary influence spreads out through the family, and through his many literary friends and admirers, the greatest of which was **Fulke Greville, 1st Baron Brooke** (1554–1628), Sidney's close friend from their first day at Shrewsbury school and author of the first biography of him. Greville rose to become James's Lord Chancellor, but remains an enigmatic, offbeat figure. His sonnet sequence *Caelica* (unpublished in his lifetime) is probably contemporary with *Astrophil and Stella*, but has a raw intellectual energy nearer to Donne than Sidney. He comments sombrely on his literary legacy, 'Now, if I leave you here, I have only laid before you a glass of disquiet.'

Edmund Spenser (c.1552–99)

Though less fashionable today, Edmund Spenser was considered the finest poet of his generation, and his long pastoral allegory The Faerie Queene (1590) – 'this rustic madrigall', as he modestly called it – was the apotheosis of poetic elegance. In February 1591, the Queen granted him an annuity of £50 for life ('All this for a song?' muttered the parsimonious Lord Burghley).

His origins are uncertain. He was a pupil at Merchant Taylors' School in London, and may have been the son of a London haberdasher, John Spenser. He claimed kinship to 'an house of auncient fame', undoubtedly a reference to the Spensers of Althorp. The fact that he was a 'sizar' at Cambridge – a student who performed menial tasks in return for free 'sizes' or rations – shows he was not rich. In the late 1570s he lived in Westminster, and was part of the 'Areopagus', a loose coterie of poets that included Sidney, Sir Edward Dyer and Gabriel Harvey. In Westminster he married his first wife, Maccabaeus Childe, whose name suggests Puritan origins.

Spenser spent much of his working life in Ireland, a dangerous colonial outpost. There he combined the duties of a middle-ranking Elizabethan civil servant with an almost mystical love of the Irish landscape. His home was Kilcolman Castle, with a 3,000-acre estate looking across to the Ballyhoura hills. There he spent tranquil days 'amongst the cooling shade/Of the green alders by Mulla's shore', and entertained Sir Walter Ralegh – the 'Shepherd of the Ocean' – who was an important patron. In Ireland he met Elizabeth Boyle, celebrated in his Amoretti sonnets; she became his second wife in 1594.

Spenser's poems have a strong vein of political and religious comment. Mother Hubberd's Tale (1591) was banned: 'though this

Edmund Spenser
Benjamin Wilson, c.1771
Spenser's monument in
Westminster Abbey, erected
in 1620, calls him the 'Prince
of Poets in his time, whose
divine spirit needs no other
witness than the works which
he left behind him'. William
Beeston, son of Shakespeare's
colleague Christopher Beeston,
gave this description of him:
'He was a little man, wore short
hair, little band [i.e. collar]
and little cuffs'.

be a jest, yet is it taken in such earnest that the book is by superior
authority called in', and the poet is 'in hazard to lose his foresaid
annual reward' (letter of Sir Thomas Tresham, 19 March 1591).
Thomas Middleton refers to Mother Hubberd 'spurting froth
upon courtiers' noses' (*The Black Book*, 1604).

Spenser was heartbroken when Kilcolman was burned
by Irish rebels in 1598. He lived his last years at Westminster
in desperate straits. He 'died for want of bread in King Street,'
according to Ben Jonson. He 'refused 20 pieces sent to him
by my Lord of Essex, and said he was sorry he had no time
to spend them'. He was buried at Westminster Abbey, close to
the river apostrophised in his famous line from *Epithalamion*:
'Sweet Thames, run softly till I end my song.'

George Chapman (c.1559–1634)

George Chapman has a place in literary folklore as the translator whose work inspired Keats's sonnet 'On First Looking into Chapman's Homer'. He was a learned and philosophical writer, but also a versatile one. He penned some mordant stage comedies, including *An Humorous Day's Mirth* (1597), which predates Jonson's 'humours' comedies, and *The Old Joiner of Aldgate* (1602), which was based on real-life Londoners and embroiled him in a lawsuit.

Despite his scholarly and often obscure poetry, Chapman was not a university man. He was born at Hitchin, Hertfordshire; his reputed birthplace on Tilehouse Street was still standing in the early twentieth century. His father, Thomas Chapman, is described as a 'yeoman' and his maternal grandfather, George Nodes, had been one of Henry VIII's kennel-masters. In his youth Chapman served Sir Ralph Sadler, Lord Lieutenant of Hertfordshire, and travelled 'beyond sea'. Like Jonson he probably saw military action in the Low Countries – a list of English soldiers recuperating in a hospital at Middleburg in 1586 includes a certain 'Joris Schampen', which may be a garbled Dutch version of his name. One of his poems includes a description of the siege of Nijmegen (1591), which he may have experienced at first hand.

Chapman's first published work was *The Shadow of Night* (1594), a compelling but opaque poem on a theme of occult nocturnal inspiration. It is prefaced with a letter to the poet Matthew Roydon, who shares his 'exceeding rapture in the deep search of knowledge'. Chapman also knew Marlowe, who (he later claimed) read *The Shadow of Night* in manuscript

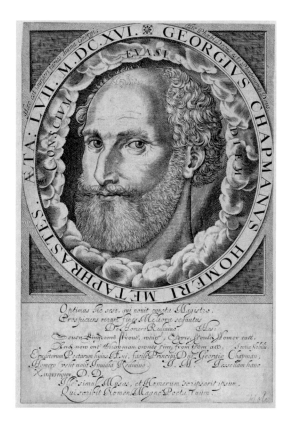

George Chapman
William Hole after an unknown
artist, published 1616

and urged him to publish it. In 1598 Chapman published
a continuation of Marlowe's unfinished *Hero and Leander*.

His translation of Homer was an intermittent labour over
nearly twenty years – he had already published part of the *Iliad* in
1598, but the complete set of Chapman's Homer comprises the
Iliad (1609), the *Odyssey* (1614–15), and the *Whole Works*, including
shorter poems (*c.*1616). These are careful – Chapman had taught
himself Greek – but not literal translations. He relates these
immense epics in his own voice, and adds digressions and
interpolations in his slightly over-bearing style. Chapman's
long, prolific, debt-ridden career seems a triumph of self-belief.

Michael Drayton (1563–1631)

A Warwickshire man, like Shakespeare, Michael Drayton described himself as 'nobly bred' and 'well allied'. This referred not to his family, of which nothing certain is known, but to his boyhood in the household of Sir Henry Goodere of Powlesworth, where he was perhaps a pageboy. According to John Aubrey, his father was a butcher, but Aubrey said the same about Shakespeare's father, who was actually a glover. A more recent conjecture is that he was son of a tanner, William Drayton, who died c.1616.

'Golden-mouthed Drayton' was widely admired, not just as a poet but as a man of integrity. 'Among scholars, soldiers, poets and all sorts of people [he] is held for a man of virtuous disposition, honest conversation, and well-governed carriage' (Francis Meres, *Palladis Tamia*, 1598). He was a plain-speaking, somewhat reclusive man. Of publishers he wrote, 'They are a company of base knaves whom I both scorn and kick at'. He wrote passionate love poems – including the famous sonnet 'Since there's no help, come let us kiss and part' – but remained a bachelor. A single unhappy passion seems to have dominated his personal life. The object of his affections (possibly his patron's daughter, Anne Goodere) is hymned for over thirty years, from the sonnets of *Idea* (1593) to the verse-epistle 'Of His Lady's Not Coming to Town' (1627).

Drayton's most famous poem was *Poly-Olbion* (1st part 1613, 2nd part 1622), an immense 'chorographical' – i.e. topographical

Æ: SVÆ, 36.   A.D. 1599.

– description of Britain's 'tracts, rivers, mountains, forests' and other features. He was already 'penning' the poem in 1598, according to Meres, so it took him at least twenty-four years to complete. He died in London, leaving a modest estate of £24 2s 8d, and was buried with honours at Westminster Abbey.

Among Drayton's friends were Francis Beaumont, William Drummond and the poet and physician Thomas Lodge, and he was often the guest of Sir John Harington at the family seat in Somerset, Kelston House. He consulted Shakespeare's son-in-law, Dr John Hall, who records curing him of a fever with an emetic syrup of violets which 'wrought very well both upwards and downwards'. Drayton is said to have dined with Shakespeare shortly before the latter's death.

His relations with Ben Jonson were difficult – he shared something of Jonson's truculence. Jonson told Drummond that 'Drayton feared him, and he esteemed not of him', but later he sublimated these tensions into a fine poem, 'The Vision of Ben Jonson, on the Muses of His Friend M. Drayton' (1627):

> It hath been questioned, Michael, if I be
> A friend at all, or if at all, to thee,
> Because who make the question have not seen
> Those ambling visits pass in verse between
> Thy muse and mine, as they expect. 'Tis true:
> You have not writ to me, nor I to you;
> And though I now begin, 'tis not to rub
> Haunch against haunch, or rise rhyming club
> About the town. This reckoning I will pay … .

The painting in the National Portrait Gallery, reproduced here, shows a rather pale, sensitive-looking man, with auburn hair and a poet's symbolic garland of laurel (whence 'laureate'). The identification of the sitter as Drayton was first suggested by Lady Mary Thompson, the picture's owner in the nineteenth century. The dates of the inscription fit, and the features are certainly comparable to the older, sterner-looking Drayton seen in a portrait by William Hole, engraved in 1613 and first published in the 1619 edition of Drayton's poems.

....

John Donne

Unknown artist, c.1595

According to Izaak Walton, Donne was 'of stature moderately tall, of a straight and equally proportioned body, to which all his words and actions gave an inexpressible addition of comeliness' (*Life of Donne*, 1681). This superb, raffish portrait of him as melancholy lover dates from the mid-1590s. In his will he left it to Robert, Earl of Ancrum, describing it as 'that picture of mine taken in the shadows'; it descended directly to its present owner, the Marquis of Lothian, but was not identified as a portrait of Donne until 1959, having been mislabelled as a portrait of the medieval scholiast Duns Scotus.

John Donne (1572–1631)

If the chivalrous soldier-poet Philip Sidney was the
Elizabethan idea of the perfect all-rounder, John Donne is
perhaps a more modern version, with his mix of intellectual
rigour and sexual passion, and his evolution from the cynical
philanderer of the *Songs and Sonnets* to the great meditator
on sin and redemption in the sermons he preached at
St Paul's Cathedral.

Donne was born into a fervently Catholic family: his
mother was a relative of Sir Thomas More and a sister of the
Jesuit leader Jasper Heywood. The family lived on Bread Street,
London, close to the Mermaid tavern. Donne's father, an
ironmonger, died when he was four and his mother married a
Catholic physician, Dr John Syminges. As a 'recusant' (literally
a refuser, i.e. a Catholic), Donne was able to study at university
but not to take a degree. He went up to Hart Hall, Oxford, in
1582, and probably studied at Cambridge as well. At twenty he
was admitted to Lincoln's Inn, nominally to study law but also
to cultivate himself as a poet, wit and man-about-town, since the
Inns of Court were a kind of 'finishing school' for young men.

Donne's earliest surviving poems, the *Satires*, date from
the mid-1590s. They are acerbic and topical but already written
in his characteristic knotty style. Their darkness seems to relate
to a period of spiritual and psychological angst when Donne
renounced his Catholicism. His younger brother Henry had
been arrested in 1593 for harbouring Catholic priests and
died in prison. An almost obsesssive theme of infidelity
runs through his secular love poetry:

Rob me but bind me not, and let me go.
Must I who come to travail thorough you
Grow your fixed subject because you are true?

In 1596 Donne was among the gentlemen-adventurers
who sailed with Essex's squadron in the famous assault on Cádiz,
and in 1597 he was at sea again in the Azores expedition under
Ralegh. On this voyage he sent his verse-letters, 'The Calm' and
'The Storm', to his Inns of Court friend Christopher Brooke. His
career prospered: he became secretary to Sir Thomas Egerton,
Lord Keeper of the Great Seal, and entered Parliament in 1601
as MP for Brackley.

At the end of that year he secretly married Lady Egerton's
seventeen-year-old niece, Ann More, and was as a result
summarily dismissed from service. He commemorated his fall
in the famous doggerel, 'John Donne/Ann Donne/Undonne'.
For some years the couple lived a threadbare life in a cottage
in Mitcham, Surrey, producing children at an alarming rate
(Ann died giving birth to their twelfth child in 1617). He was
supported by various patrons, notably Sir Robert Drury of
Hawstead, Suffolk, but remained in a kind of social wilderness.
His verse darkened and grew more religious: the *Holy Sonnets*
(c.1610–11) and *Anniversaries* (1612–13).

Despite their intellectual difficulty, the poems have a
marvellously direct, conversational, almost buttonholing tone.
Many of them existed only in manuscript copies sent to friends,
and when he was contemplating a printed edition, in about 1614,
Donne had to collect them back in – 'by this occasion I am made
a rhapsoder of mine own rags, and that cost me more diligence
to seek them than it did to write them'. In the event they

John Donne
Unknown artist after Isaac
Oliver's miniature of 1616
This portrait, a copy of a
miniature by Isaac Oliver
dated 1616 (Royal Collection),
shows Donne at this time:
a sharp-bearded, punctilious-
looking man in his forties.
The expression seems to be
edged with disappointment

remained unpublished during his lifetime: the first collection
was issued in 1633.

In 1615 Donne took holy orders, and King James (who seems
to have considered him untrustworthy in political matters) made
him chaplain-in-ordinary to the royal household. He became Dr
Donne by virtue of a Doctorate of Divinity awarded by Cambridge
University, though this was at the King's insistence; indeed, an
overtone of careerism hangs over Donne's entry into the Church.
When his wife died he preached her funeral sermon at St Clement
Danes in London. Walton recalled: 'His very looks and words ...
did so work upon the affections of his hearers, as melted and
moulded them into a companionable sadness'. In 1621, through
the offices of the Duke of Buckingham, the King's favourite,
Donne was made Dean of St Paul's. The greatest preacher of his
day, his most famous sermon begins 'No man is an island ...'.

Edward de Vere, 17th Earl of Oxford (1550–1604)

Though the Earl of Oxford has been claimed by some as the author of Shakespeare's plays, his literary output was in fact aristocratically slight. The few poems that are definitely his are clever, melodious and shallow. There seems no reason (other than pure snobbery) to assign to him the breadths and profundities of Shakespeare's writing.

Like the Howards and the Percys, the de Veres were pedigree Catholics. Orphaned young, Edward was brought up under the watchful guardianship of Lord Burghley. In 1567 he killed one of Burghley's servants, a cook named Brincknell, but was acquitted on an absurd plea that Brincknell had committed suicide by 'running upon' the Earl's sword.

At twenty-five he embarked on a long and lavish Grand Tour. In just over a year he spent £5,000 and 'lived in Florence in more grandeur than the Duke of Tuscany' (John Aubrey). After his return, he became a byword for fashionable Italianate affectations. In 1579 the Cambridge don Gabriel Harvey tilted at him in a satire, 'Speculum Tuscanismi'. This was reported to Oxford by his secretary, the author John Lyly, an enemy of Harvey's.

Oxford seemed destined for high office – especially after marrying Burghley's daughter – but he was capricious and unstable. In 1579 he quarrelled with Sir Philip Sidney during a tennis game,

....
OPPOSITE
Edward de Vere, 17th Earl of Oxford
Unknown artist, seventeenth century, after an original of 1575
The portrait here shows the Earl as he might have looked around the age of thirty, sumptuously decked out in shades of moleskin-grey and tangerine-red. He is haughty, fastidious and faintly repellent.

calling him 'puppy' and threatening to kill him. He was also jealous of Ralegh, who was briefly associated with the Oxford set.

In 1580 he left his wife and daughter when his mistress, courtly acolyte Anne Vavasour, had a child. That year the Earl of Arundel affirmed, 'I will prove him a buggerer of a boy that is his cook.' Oxford was also accused of wild atheistic rants, such as calling the Virgin Mary a whore and Joseph a cuckold. All in all, an air of squandered brilliance hangs over his life.

Sir John Harington (1561–1612)

The poet and wit Sir John Harington was the Queen's godson.
His father, John, was a confidant of Henry VIII, married one of the
king's illegitimate daughters, Etheldreda Malte, and cultivated a
close relationship with Princess Elizabeth which was rewarded
when she came to the throne. The younger Harington studied at
Eton and King's College, Cambridge, and later at Lincoln's Inn.
He was popular at court, a noted epigrammist and a risqué
conversationalist – a kind of intellectual jester.

Harington's fine translation of the Italian epic *Orlando Furioso* was
published in 1591. According to tradition, he first translated some
erotic passages, and circulated them at court, whereupon the Queen
made him translate the rest as a penance. His much-loved dog, Bungey,
features on the decorated title-page. In 1596 Harington published
The Metamorphosis of Ajax. This curious book – part burlesque, part
technical manual – is essentially a treatise on the design of lavatories
(Ajax puns on a 'jakes', or privy). Banished once more from court as
a result of this publication, he retired to his Somerset home, Kelston
House, near Bath. He threw in his lot with the Earl of Essex (see page
10), went with him to Ireland in 1598 and was knighted by him. But
he steered a skilful course between the Queen and the overreaching
Earl, and so (as he put it) escaped 'shipwreck on the Essex coast'.

The Queen called him 'that saucy poet, my godson' and forgave
him effronteries that others would not have dared to attempt. His
cousin Robert Markham warned him, 'That damnable uncovered
honesty of yours will mar your fortune.' His miscellaneous writings,
Nugae Antiquae, were collected by a descendant, the Reverend Henry
Harington, and published between 1769 and 1774. They display
an elegant, observant, inquisitive mind.

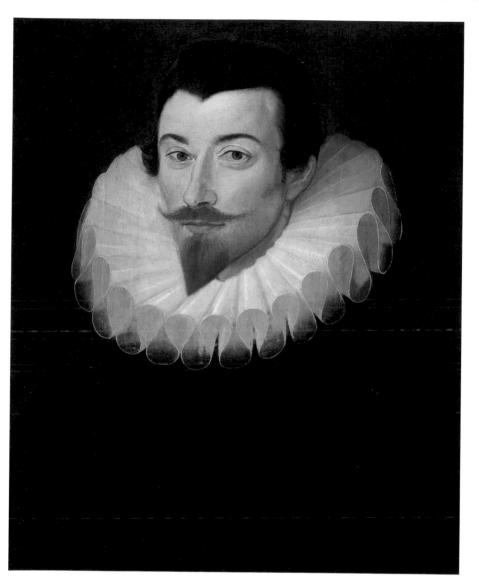

Sir John Harington
attributed to Hieronimo Custodis, c.1590–5
This portrait catches the mordant courtly joker, with his thin
laconic mouth and his sharp-pointed *pic-à-devant* beard.

Maids of Honour

No account of Elizabeth's court is complete without a mention of that bevy of well-born, sparky and glamorous young women known as the Queen's Maids of Honour. Some are particularly associated with the poets and dramatists of the period – as muses, mistresses and indeed wives.

Under the tutelage of a formidable Welsh spinster, Blanche Parry, the Maids served the Queen's more intimate needs, attended her at court functions and performed in court masques. There were generally six Maids of Honour at any time, quartered in the 'Maidens' chamber', though the turnover was high. They were royal servants, but the word 'Maids' indicates also their virginal status, as befits the cultish imagery of Elizabeth as the 'Virgin Queen'. The reality was, of course, rather different, and their many scandalous liaisons were a staple of court gossip.

Yorkshire-born **Anne Vavasour** (fl.1580–1621) had a career more rackety than most. Within a few months of being enrolled as a Maid in 1580 she was pregnant by the volatile Earl of Oxford; their son was born in March 1581 (see page 71). The Queen took an exceedingly dim view of such breaches of maidenly etiquette and the lovers were dispatched briefly to the Tower. Their son, christened Edward Vere, went on to a distinguished military career. Various poems exist on the affair. A manuscript now in the Folger Library in Washington attributes two of them – 'Though I seem strange, sweet friend' and 'Sitting alone upon my thought' – to Anne herself. Her later career included a long liaison with the Queen's Champion at tilt, Sir Henry Lee (see page 13), by whom she had another illegitimate son. She married twice. The second contract, to one John Richardson, was technically bigamous, as her estranged first husband, John Finch, was still alive. She was prosecuted for bigamy by Sir Henry Lee's son, who hoped thereby to wrest from her an inheritance settled on her by Lee at his death in 1611. The prosecution was successful and in 1621 the Court of High Commission sentenced her to a ruinous fine of £2,000 – the last-known documentation of her life.

Mary (or Mal) Fitton (1578–1641), daughter of Sir Edward Fitton, became a Maid of Honour in the late 1590s. The Comptroller of the royal household, Sir William Knollys, promised her father that he would be a 'good shepherd' to her and 'defend the innocent lamb from the wolvish cruelty' of the court. However, the upshot was that he fell head over heels in love with her, as he confided in a series of surprisingly frank letters to her sister, Anne Newdigate. Knollys was a married man in his fifties, of Puritan persuasion, and his infatuation was grist to the mill of court humorists. According to one hypothesis, the aged suitor was guyed as Malvolio ('I want Mal') in Shakespeare's Twelfth Night, performed at court during the Christmas festivities of 1600–1. Mary herself, meanwhile, embarked on an affair with William Herbert, 3rd Earl of Pembroke, and in early 1601 she was pregnant by him; Knollys wrote furiously about this 'man of sin … having in the night sowed tares amongst the good corn'. According to a contemporary letter-writer, 'when … the Earl of Pembroke favoured her, she would tuck up her clothes, put on a white cloak, and march out of the court like a man to meet him' (further shades of Twelfth Night). Mary gave birth to a son who died shortly after, and by the end of 1601 she had left court under a cloud. For all their personal

charms – visible in their sumptuous portraits – Vavasour and
Fitton suggest the vulnerabilities of the Maids in a predatory court.
Observers noted Mal's melancholy disposition.

Bess Throckmorton (1565–1647) was a woman of a rather
different stamp. The Throckmortons were a powerful family of
political servants. Her father, Sir Nicholas Throckmorton, served
Elizabeth as ambassador in both France and Scotland, but there
was also a fractious element in the family. One of Bess's cousins
was Francis Throckmorton, the Catholic conspirator executed in
1584; another, on the other side of the religious spectrum, was Job
Throckmorton, the abettor (and in some views the author) of the
brilliantly ribald anti-episcopal pamphlets issued under the alias
'Martin Marprelate'. Like Vavasour and Fitton, Bess became famous
because of an illicit pregnancy, though unlike them the father,

Lady Ralegh (Elizabeth Throckmorton)
English School, sixteenth century

Frances Howard, Countess of Somerset (detail)
attributed to William Larkin, c.1615

Sir Walter Ralegh, did the honourable thing and married her.
(A scurrilous anecdote by John Aubrey refers to Ralegh 'getting
up one of the Maids of Honour up against a tree', but this seems to
be another woman). Their secret marriage took place in November
1591. Despite the Queen's predictable displeasure the marriage
stood (though their son Damerei died early) and they set up home
in rustic exile in Sherborne, Dorset. Bess bore him two more
sons, Wat and Carew, and remained his faithful supporter during
his long years of imprisonment in the Tower (1603–16).

For some the brush with the ladies of the court proved
fatal, as in the case of the minor litterateur Sir Thomas Overbury.
Overbury is remembered less for his literary attainments than
for his death by poison in the Tower of London. He had risen on
the coat-tails of King James's favourite Robert Carr (see page 20),
whose intimate friend he was, but they then fell out over Carr's

A man's best fortune or his worst's a wife:
Yet J, that knew nor mariage peace nor strife,
Live by a good, by a bad one lost my life.
A wife like her J writ, man scarse can wed:
Of a false friend like mine, man scarse hath red.

controversial marriage to the voluptuous Frances Howard. She was accounted the most beautiful and dangerous lady in the land, and had shocked polite society by divorcing the 3rd Earl of Essex on the grounds of his impotence. (She had undergone a virginity test, though the general opinion on that was summed up by the Prince of Wales, who refused to pick up her glove from the dance floor, saying 'it had been stretched' by too many others.) The couple then proceeded to engineer Overbury's imprisonment in the Tower, where he was slowly poisoned by doctors and apothecaries in their pay. The *coup de grâce* was 'a clyster [enema] of corrosive sublimate' that was administered to him on 14 September 1613; he died early the following day. Much about the case remains mysterious. The Carrs were convicted of conspiracy to murder but were pardoned; four lesser accomplices — including the 'cunning-woman' and court madame, Anne Turner — were executed in 1615.

Pamphleteers

Far from the court, living in rented rooms 'at the town's end', haunted by debt and imprisonment, the pamphleteers of the day dashed off satires, romances and entertainingly digressive essays. They were professional writers, but lived precariously in an age that knew no copyright. A typical one-off payment for a pamphlet was £2 ('forty shillings and an odd pottle of wine'), with perhaps the same again for a fawning dedication to some well-breeched patron.

Among this 'riff-raff of the scribbling rascality' was one of the finest comic-prose writers of any age, **Thomas Nashe** (1567–c.1601). A parson's son from Lowestoft, Suffolk, he was a sizar scholar at St John's College, Cambridge. He left university in 1588 and won popularity with works such as Pierce Penniless (1592) and The Unfortunate Traveller (1594). The latter, a picaresque tale narrated by the roguish pageboy Jack Wilton, is sometimes canvassed as the first 'novel' in English. Much of Nashe's energies were expended in controversy – 'let me but touch a piece of paper, there arise such storms and tempests about my ears' – but he was more than an entertaining mud-slinger. He was a journalist avant la lettre and is valued today for those veins of reportage, of casual topicality, that make his writings a 'granary for commentators'.

In 1597 Nashe left London hurriedly when his comedy The Isle of Dogs, co-written with Ben Jonson, was adjudged seditious by the Privy Council. He surfaced a few months later in Great Yarmouth, where he wrote his last and most idiosyncratic work, Nashe's Lenten Stuffe (1599). Its subtitle, 'The Praise of the Red Herring', is both literal (red herrings, or kippers, were a staple of Yarmouth) and metaphorical. The work is an almost surreal

The trimming of Thomas Nashe.

But see, what art thou heere? *lupus* in *fabula*, a lop in a chaine? Nowe sirra haue at you, th'art in my swinge. But soft, fetterd? thou art out againe: I cannot come neere thee, thou hast a charme about thy legges, *no man meddle with the Queenes prisoner*, now therefore let vs talke freendlye, and as *Alexander* sayd to hys Father *Phillip*, who beeing sorely wounded in the thigh in fight, and hardly escaping death, but could
E 2   not

GREENE IN CONCEIPT.

New raised from his graue to write the Tragique Historie of faire *Valeria* of London.

WHEREIN IS TRVLY DISCOVERED the rare and lamentable issue of a Husbands dotage, a wiues leudnesse, & childrens disobedience,

Received and reported by I.D.

Veritas non quærit angulos, vmbra gaudet.

Printed at London by RICHARD BRADOCKE for *William Iones*, dwelling at the signe of the Gunne neare Holborne conduit. 1598.

....
ABOVE LEFT
Thomas Nashe
Unknown engraver, published 1597
Among Nashe's many enemies was a barber-surgeon from Cambridge, Richard Lichfield, whose pamphlet *The Trimming of Thomas Nashe* includes this image of him fettered in irons. Though such woodcuts are often generalised, its features are corroborated by verbal descriptions of Nashe as a skinny, boyish and (unusually for an Elizabethan) beardless figure: even his goofy 'gag teeth', mentioned by Harvey, seem to be represented.

....
ABOVE RIGHT
Robert Greene
Unknown engraver, published 1598
Though fanciful as a portrait, this posthumous woodcut from the title page of John Dickenson's *Greene in Conceipt* showing the ghost of Robert Greene gives a neat visual synopsis of the tools of the pamphleteer's trade: pen, notebook, ink-well, paper-knife.

....
Gabriel Harvey
Unknown engraver, published 1596
This image of Harvey appears in Nashe's salvo against him, *Have with you to Saffron Walden*, where it is captioned, 'Gabriel Harvey as he is about to let fly upon Ajax', a quibble on 'jakes', or privy.

tissue of tangential 'red herrings' that seems to anticipate writers such as Laurence Sterne and James Joyce.

Nashe's first mentor in London was another university man, the flamboyant, red-bearded **Robert Greene** (c.1558–92). At Cambridge, Greene recalled, 'I ruffled out in my silks in the habit of malcontent' – an idea that appealed also to Marlowe, whose heretical scholar Dr Faustus wished to 'fill the public schools with silk'. Greene made his name in the 1580s as a penner of 'love pamphlets' – the light reading of the day: 'dainty' fare 'to stuff serving-men's pockets', as Nashe put it. One of these, *Pandosto* (1588), later provided the plot-line for Shakespeare's *Winter's Tale*, though in his lifetime Greene was

bitterly jealous of the young Shakespeare. Among his last
works were 'coney-catching' pamphlets, detailing the wiles
of Elizabethan con-men and cut-purses (a 'coney' or rabbit
was slang for a dupe). It was a world he knew well: his
mistress was the sister of a thief called 'Cutting' Ball,
who was hanged at Tyburn.

Greene died at his last lodgings, a shoemaker's house
in Dowgate, in September 1592. A gloating account of his
death was instantly published by **Gabriel Harvey** (c.1550–1631),
a Cambridge don, a friend of Spenser and the self-appointed
scourge of the 'liberties' of the popular press. According to
Dr Harvey, Greene had over-indulged at a 'feast' of pickled
herrings and Rhenish wine with Nashe and had died 'pitifully',
in a lice-infested bed, calling for a 'penny pot of Malmesey'.
These comments aroused the fury of Nashe, who attacked him
in Strange News (1592), and Have with you to Saffron Walden (1596),
which includes a wonderful mock-biography. Harvey's replies,
such as Pierce's Supererogation (1593), are pompous and unwieldy,
and tend to justify Nashe's description of him as an 'indigested
chaos of doctorship and greedy pot-hunter after applause'.

This 'civil war of wits' fostered a glut of satirical writings
in the later 1590s. On 1 June 1599 the Archbishop of Canterbury
issued a decree banning various 'unseemly satires', including
'all Nashe's books and Dr Harvey's books'. On 4 June some books
'thereupon were burnt' at Stationers' Hall. Within a couple of
years Nashe was dead, still in his early thirties. Ben Jonson wrote
an elegy (discovered in the archives of Berkeley Castle in 1995) in
which he speaks warmly of his 'dear friend' and fears his death
will provoke 'a general dearth of wit throughout this land'.
Having retired to his native Saffron Walden, Harvey lived to

IOANNES FLORIVS AVGVSTÆ ANNÆ ANGL: SCOT: FRANC: ET HIB: REGINÆ PRÆLECTOR LING: ITALICÆ

ÆT: 58. A: D: 1611.

CHI SI CONTENTA GODE

En virtute suâ contentus, nobilis arte,
Italus ore, Anglus pectore, uterq̃ opere.
Floret adhuc, et adhuc florebit; floreat ultra
FLORIVS, hâc specie floridus, optat amans.

Gul: Hole sculp:

Tam fœlix utinam.

a great age, annotating his vast library: his marginalia alone
fill a book, probably his best.

An unexpected vein of reportage is also found in the
language-manuals of the day, designed for learners of (mainly)
French and Italian. The conventional format featured short
dialogues and scenes, which in skilled hands became rich
vignettes of Elizabethan life. John Eliot's French manual, *Ortho-
epia Gallica* (1593), is one of the most colourful – a 'fantastical
rhapsody of dialogism', as he calls it, with sketches of city life
under such titles as 'The Apothecary', 'The Pawn', 'Dicing', etc.
The best-known of these language-teachers was **John Florio**
(1553–1625), the English-born son of an Italian Protestant
refugee. His Italian manual, *Florio's Second Fruits* (1591), is in
the same lively mould. Florio was a tutor of the young Earl of
Southampton, which has caused speculation about his relations
with Shakespeare. It is unlikely that the pedant Holofernes
in *Love's Labours Lost* is a caricature, though it is certainly true
that Holofernes quotes from Florio's compendium of Italian
proverbs, the *Garden of Recreation* (1591). Florio's greatest works
were an English translation of Montaigne's *Essays* (1603),
which Shakespeare also knew and used, and his great
Italian–English dictionary.

....

OPPOSITE
John Florio
William Hole, published 1611
The second edition of Florio's Italian–English dictionary (1611) contains over 70,000 entries
and features this engraved portrait by William Hole. Sir William Cornwallis described Florio
as 'a fellow less beholding to Nature ... for his face than his fortune' (*Essayes*, 1600). He seems
to mean that Florio was ugly; the portrait does not bear this out, though close inspection
reveals what appear to be some pimples or boils on the right side of his face.

Travel Writers

A fascination with travel and discovery percolates richly into the literature of the day, from the exotic itineraries of Marlowe's *Tamburlaine* – 'I crossed the sea and came to Oblia,/And Negra Silva where the devils dance ...' – to Falstaff's hope that the merry wife he is pursuing will be 'a region in Guiana, all gold and bounty'. The romance-writer Thomas Lodge actually wrote at sea: his *Rosalynde* (1590) was composed during a privateering voyage to the Canaries, every page 'hatched in the storms of the ocean, and feathered in the surges of many perilous seas'. A later journey to South America resulted in *A Marguerite of America* (1596), featuring an Inca princess. Shakespeare draws on New World expeditions in *The Tempest*, echoing accounts of the wreck of the *Sea-Adventurer* in Bermuda (Shakespeare's 'still-vexed Bermoothes') in 1609.

These are literary responses to Elizabethan and Jacobean travel but they are not travel literature. The latter, as a genre, was in its infancy and much that was published (for example, in *Principal Navigations*, Richard Hakluyt's great collection of 1589) was brisk and bland – log-books rather than literature. An important exception is the marvellously observant and detailed account of native American life by **Thomas Harriot** (c.1560–1621). He was part of the Virginia expedition of 1585 that established the ill-fated English colony at Roanoke. He was 'employed in discovering', as he put it, and his *Brief Discourse of Virginia* (1588) provides unprecedented insight into the culture and customs of the Algonquin Indians. Harriot's mentor Ralegh also contributed to this anthropological branch of Elizabethan literature with his *Discovery of Guiana* (1596), narrating his expedition in search of the fabled 'golden city' of El Dorado.

AN. DNI 1602 .
ÆTATIS SVÆ 3 2

Possibly Thomas Harriot
Unknown artist, 1602

The career of **Sir Robert Dudley** (1574–1649), illegitimate
son of the Earl of Leicester, provides a picturesque example of an
Englishman with the travel bug. In 1595, he sailed the Caribbean in
search of prizes; his exploration of the lower Orinoco, the supposed
gateway to El Dorado, predates Ralegh's more famous venture by
a few weeks. In 1603, frustrated in his attempts to establish his
legitimacy, Dudley eloped to the Continent with a Maid of Honour,
Elizabeth Southwell. He entered the service of the Medici Dukes
of Tuscany and lived in Florence for many years; his fortifications
can still be seen at Livorno. In 1646 he published his masterwork,

the six books entitled *Dell' arcano del mare* (The Secrets of the Sea), but much of his writing remains in manuscript.

The Shakespearian contemporary who best fits the term 'travel writer' is the eccentric **Thomas Coryate** (1576–1617). He was born in Odcombe, Somerset, and referred to himself as the 'Odcombian Leg-stretcher'. He had, and still has, a paradoxical reputation. On the one hand, he was a kind of comedian or learned buffoon, an 'anvil' for courtly wits. On the other, he was the tough and courageous traveller whose journeys in Europe and Asia were the more remarkable for being almost entirely done on foot. Both these reputations were diligently cultivated by Coryate himself, who was also a great self-publicist.

In 1608, at the age of thirty-two, he set out on the European journey that made his name. 'There hath itched a very burning desire in me,' he wrote, 'to survey and contemplate some of the chiefest parts of this goodly fabric of the world.' By his own estimate, he covered 1,975 miles in a little over five months and visited forty-five cities. He then settled back in his study at Odcombe and painstakingly relived the journey on paper. The resulting book, *Coryate's Crudities*, took him three years and the first edition runs to 654 pages. Its full title is itself a masterpiece: 'Coryate's Crudities, Hastily gobled up in five Moneths travells in France, Savoy, Italy, Rhetia commonly called the Grisons country, Helvetia alias Switzerland, some parts of High Germany and the Netherlands; Newly digested in the hungry aire of Odcombe in the County of Somerset, and now dispersed to the nourishment of the travelling members of this Kingdome.'

....
OPPOSITE
Sir Robert Dudley, Earl of Warwick
attributed to Nicholas Hilliard, c.1591–3

Loe heere the wooden Image of our wits;
Borne, in firſt trauaile, on the backs of Nits;
But now on Elephants, &c:
O, what will he ride, when his yeares expire?
The world muſt ride him; or he all will tire.

'Crudities' is to be taken in the French sense, *crudités* –
pieces of raw food, or in this case raw experience, 'hastily
gobbled up' on the journey and now 'digested' back home and
'dispersed' to his readers. The metaphor inescapably suggests
the travel book as a kind of post-prandial fart, a motif continued
by the sequel, the *Crambe Biscoctum* (Twice-cooked Cabbage),
also published in 1611.

The *Crudities* is a triumph of self-advertisement but
has more solid virtues too. After the extended badinage of
the prefatory matter (to which his friends Donne and Jonson
contributed) the actual travelogue is delivered in a direct,
unfussy style. Jonson aptly calls Coryate a 'bold carpenter of
words'. Much of the text is practical, indeed statistical (journey

times, populations, dimensions of notable buildings, etc.). Travellers carried it with them as a *vade mecum* or guidebook. Coryate himself met the adventurer Sir Robert Shirley in the hinterlands of Persia and was delighted when he drew forth from his luggage 'both my books neatly kept'.

He set out on his last great journey in 1612 and after three years of ferocious 'leg-stretching' was in India. At Ajmer on 22 December 1615 he was among the reception committee for the first English ambassador, Sir Thomas Roe. He insisted on greeting the exhausted Roe – who was, in his own words, 'scarce a crow's dinner' – with a long oration. Roe describes him in his journal as 'the famous unwearied walker, Tho. Coryatt, who on foot had passed most of Europe and Asia and was now in India, being but the beginning of his travels'. The nonchalant flourish at the end sounds like a Coryate catch-phrase echoed verbatim.

Coryate's last writings are newsletters sent from India. One is addressed to the 'Fraternity of Sireniacal Gentlemen that meet the first Friday of every month at the sign of the Mermaid in Bread Street' – the only documentary reference to the much-bruited Mermaid 'club'. These letters were printed up in a short pamphlet, *Thomas Coriate, Traveller for the English Witts: Greeting* (1616), with a woodcut of Coryate riding an elephant. The text of his 'oration' to the Mughal emperor Jahangir is given in both Persian and English. He says, 'I am a poor traveller and world-seer, which am come hither from a far country.' In the original Persian, Coryate uses the word *fakir* to describe himself, and to this day he is remembered in India as the 'English fakir'. He died at Surat, north of Bombay, in 1617.

Scientists

'In those dark times,' wrote John Aubrey apropos the Elizabethan scientist Thomas Allen, 'astrologer, mathematician and conjuror were accounted the same things, and the vulgar did verily believe him to be a conjuror.' This conveys the difficulties of the scientist in the Shakespearian age. Experimental science was still entangled with metaphysical and magical aspirations, and was hampered by suspicions of doctrinal heresy. The era of empiricism was only just dawning, the great figures of seventeenth-century science – Isaac Newton, Robert Boyle, Robert Hooke, etc. – unborn in Shakespeare's lifetime.

The most famous and prolific of the Elizabethan scientist-magicians was **John Dee** (c.1527–1608), who wrote nearly eighty books. He is better known for his magical pursuits, but any serious account of Dee must include his influential 'Mathematicall Preface' to Sir Henry Billingsley's translation of Euclid (1570) and his *General and Rare Memorials of Navigation* (1577), the latter a reminder that England's seafaring power was in part based on the mathematical expertise of men such as Dee.

Another important figure in this transitional period was Thomas Harriot (see page 107). He corresponded with the astronomer Kepler and designed a 'perspective trunk' that anticipates the telescope. He served the scholarly Earl of Northumberland in the Tower, where the Earl was imprisoned after the Gunpowder Plot. The Earl's Tower accounts include such items as 'To Dr Turner's man that brought a skeleton', 'Mending the globes & spheres at the Tower' and numerous payments to his distiller, Roger Cook. Another of the Earl's retainers was Walter Warner, whose theories on the circulation of blood predate those of the more famous William Harvey.

....
Dr John Dee
Unknown artist, c.1594
Despite his scientific interests, Dr Dee remains the epitome of the Elizabethan magus. His 'shew-stone', a crystal ball of polished quartz, can be seen in the British Museum, and there are voluminous transcripts of his séances or 'angelic conferences', in which his partner was the fraudulent spirit-medium Edward Kelley. 'He was tall and slender', wrote Aubrey, with 'a long beard as white as milk.'

In the natural sciences, a leading figure was the horticulturalist **John Gerard** (1545–1612), whose *Herbal* (1597) remains a landmark in botanical description and classification. Another Elizabethan naturalist was the entomologist Thomas Moffett, whose compendious *Theatre of Insects* was published in 1634; he was also a physician, championing the new 'chymicall physick' of Paracelsus. But Gerard and Moffett were unusual: the general tendency in Elizabethan natural sciences was to reiterate earlier authorites. Thus Edward Topsell's *History of Four-Footed Beasts* (1607) offered material drawn from 'Scriptures, Fathers, Philosophers, Physicians and Poets', together with 'sundry accidental Histories, Hierogliphycks, Epigrams, Emblems, and Aenigmatical Observations'.

....

John Gerard
William Rogers after an unknown
artist, published 1598
A surgeon by training, Gerard was Lord
Burghley's chief gardener and his own
garden in Holborn was famous for its
collection of 'trees, fruits and plants,
both indigenous and exotic'.

Sir Henry Wotton
Unknown artist, n.d.

This wonderfully engaging image is an old copy of a portrait at Eton that was painted in the 1630s. It shows Wotton in quizzically scholastic mode. The eyes watch us expectantly and the mouth has a thin smile of encouragement: we are almost audibly invited to debate, to challenge, or at least to amuse. The inscription reads: PHILOSOPHEMUR – 'let us philosophise'.

Sir Henry Wotton (1568–1639)

Wotton was a diplomat and dilettante whose main claim
to literary fame is the miscellany of poems, essays and 'table-talk'
collected under the title *Reliquiae Wottonianae* (1651). It radiates
charm: learned, pragmatic, sceptical.

Educated at Winchester and Oxford, he entered the service
of the Earl of Essex in 1595 (see page 10). As Essex's secretary and
intelligence-gatherer he was a rival of Anthony Bacon, brother of
Francis. Though not implicated in the Essex Rising of 1601, he left
the country to avoid recriminations. In 1602 he travelled incognito
from Florence to Scotland, under the alias Octavio Baldi, to warn
King James of a Catholic plot to poison him. He was knighted by
James in 1603, and the following year became ambassador to
Venice. He famously defined an ambassador as 'an honest man
sent to lie abroad for the good of his country'.

He held various diplomatic appointments until his retirement
in 1624. He then became provost of Eton, a post he held until his
death. He published *The Elements of Architecture* (1624), of which the
gossip John Chamberlain said, 'it is well-spoken of, though his
own castles have been in the air'.

Wotton never married. Among his close friends were John
Donne and Francis Bacon. Donne wrote to him praising the wandering
life and freedom from the 'hell' of routine: 'Be thou thine own home,
and in thy self dwell./Inn anywhere – continuance maketh hell.'

Wotton shared with Izaak Walton a passion for fishing; they
fished together a stretch of the Thames near Eton called 'Black
Pots'. Wotton wrote an account of the sport which predates Walton's
Compleat Angler. His best-known poem is 'The Character of a Happy
Life', which Ben Jonson said in 1619 he 'hath by heart'.

Sir Francis Bacon (1561–1626)

A century after Bacon's death, the poet Pope summed him up as 'the wisest, brightest, meanest of mankind'. Of his brilliance there is no doubt – the range of his intellectual concerns, the toughness and lucidity of his prose, his tireless empiricism in an age still prone to what he called the 'phantoms of the mind'. As Pope implied, however, Bacon's personality also contained elements of coldness and ruthlessness, and charges of personal treachery have been levelled at him.

Bacon's best-known works are the *Essays* (1597), *The Advancement of Learning* (1605) and *Novum Organum* (1620), but his name is more often evoked in the context of his supposed authorship of Shakespeare's plays. Bacon was the son of the powerful politician Sir Nicholas Bacon and the uncle of the painter Nathaniel Bacon. His elder brother Anthony was also gifted, but dissipated his talents in intrigue and died young of gout. In the 1590s Bacon was closely identified with the Earl of Essex's faction (see page 10), but in 1601 he was the Earl's chief prosecutor after the abortive Essex Rising. This is generally painted as a cynical volte-face, but he took part in the trial reluctantly, under heavy pressure from the Queen, and when the inevitable verdict came he was active in urging clemency

....
OPPOSITE
Francis Bacon, 1st Viscount St Alban
Unknown artist, after 1731; after an original of 1618
Bacon was described as of 'middling stature' and 'presence grave and comely', though the physician William Harvey added that he had 'the eye of a viper'. The painting here, a later copy of one at Gorhambury, shows Bacon in Chancellor's robes – the original must therefore have been painted in or after 1618. He was then in his mid-fifties, so the portrait hardly bears out Arthur Wilson's comment that 'his countenance had indented with age before he was old' (*History of Great Britain*, 1653). In this later portrait Bacon has brown hair and brown eyes, a characteristic tall black hat, and that shrewd, sceptical look which makes one think of his *Essays* – 'What is truth, said jesting Pilate, and would not stay for an answer'.

....

Francis Bacon, Viscount St Alban
Elkington & Co., cast by Dominico Brucciani after an unknown artist, c.1875
The marble tomb effigy in St Michael's Church, St Albans, illustrated here by the electrotype copy
in the National Portrait Gallery's collection, is unusual among Elizabethan and Jacobean tomb
effigies for its sense of world-weariness, even effeteness, even though its contemplative mood
seems appropriate to Bacon's 'presence grave'.

for Essex. Bacon was also involved in the trial and execution of Sir Walter Ralegh in 1618, and, as with the Essex trial, has been cast as the heartless prosecutor of Ralegh at his most tragic and charismatic.

Bacon's star rose under King James – he became Solicitor General (1607), Attorney General (1613), Lord Keeper (1617) and Lord Chancellor (1618). In 1621 a hostile Parliament charged him with corruption: specifically, taking bribes in return for favourable judgements. He admitted guilt, accepted disgrace and retired to his estate at Gorhambury, near St Albans. There he indulged his passion for gardening and wrote his strange last works, *Sylva Sylvarum* and *New Atlantis*, both published in 1627, a year after his death.

Bacon and his brother Anthony were both homosexual – Anthony was charged with buggery in France in the 1580s. In 1593 Bacon's mother complained of his intimacy with his servant Harry Percy, a 'proud, profane, costly fellow' who was his 'coach companion and bed companion'. His marriage to Alice Barnham, at the late age of forty-six, was marked by coldness and disharmony. He rewrote his will, revoking bequests to her, shortly before his death.

Lytton Strachey said that Bacon tried 'to shape, with his subtle razor-blade, the crude vague blocks of passion and fact', and ultimately failed because 'his own heart was hidden from him'. Bacon himself says something similar: 'Although our persons live in the view of heaven, yet our spirits are included in the cave of our own complexions and customs, which minister unto us infinite errors and vain opinions.'

Sir Walter Ralegh (c.1554–1618)

Ralegh was a high achiever in so many walks of Elizabethan life – courtier, soldier, philosopher, historian, scientist, parliamentarian, explorer – that his brilliance as a poet is sometimes forgotten. He was born in Devon and 'spake broad Devonshire to his dying day'. The Queen's nickname for him, 'Water', is Walter in a cod yokel accent.

A younger son of a moderately prosperous squire, Ralegh had to make his own way. He was the Elizabethan self-made man *par excellence*. The most famous piece of Ralegh folklore – the laying of his cloak in the mud for the Queen – encapsulates this. Unlike some other Ralegh legends (that he introduced tobacco to England, for instance), the cloak story has a surprising streak of authenticity. In its first guise it reads as follows:

> This Captain Ralegh, coming out of Ireland to the English court in good habit (his clothes being then a considerable part of his estate) found the Queen walking, till meeting with a plashy place, she seemed to scruple going thereon. Presently Ralegh cast and spread his new plush cloak on the ground, whereon the Queen trod gently, rewarding him afterwards with many suits, for his so free and seasonable tender of so fair a footcloth. (Thomas Fuller, *Worthies of England*, 1660)

This account is not quite contemporary, but there are documents that tend to corroborate it. Ralegh did indeed present himself at court, bearing Irish dispatches, in December 1581 (when the ground would indeed have been 'plashy' underfoot). The point of the story is not that Ralegh was obsequious, as is sometimes thought, but

....

Sir Walter Ralegh
attributed to monogrammist 'H', 1588
In this portrait we see a plush cloak on Ralegh's shoulder
and a magnificent pearl earring said to have been brought
back by the explorers he had sent to Virginia. The motto
names his twin ideals as 'love and virtue'.

that he was prepared to gamble – he did not at this point have new plush cloaks to spare: it was perhaps his only cloak which he hazarded, and which won him many 'suits' as a result.

In the 1580s Ralegh rose vertiginously through the courtly ranks: the Queen's latest amour. He was knighted on 1 January 1585, though she cannily declined to give him any real political or even landed power base. He was also at this time styled 'Lord and Governor of Virginia' – the English colony on the North American coast which he 'planted' and sponsored but never actually visited. (This is another Ralegh legend: in fact the only bit of the Americas he visited was Venezuela, in search of the ever-elusive gold of El Dorado.)

If Ralegh was a self-made man, he was also vulnerable – as all at court were – to being suddenly and drastically 'unmade' by the Queen. So it was in early 1592, when his secret marriage to Elizabeth Throckmorton was revealed; their son, Damerei, was born in March (see pages 95 and 96). After a brief spell in the Tower, the erring couple retired in disgrace to Ralegh's estate, Sherborne Castle, Dorset.

> Sir Walter Ralegh was one that it seems Fortune had picked out of purpose, of whom to make an example or to use as her tennis ball … for she tossed him up of nothing, and to and fro, and from thence down to little more than that wherein she found him, a bare gentleman.
> (Sir Robert Naunton, *Fragmenta Regalia*, 1631)

In 1593, Ralegh began work converting a Tudor hunting lodge at Sherborne into the fine mansion which, with a few later additions, one sees today. For the next ten years he lived here: a country squire's life interspersed with adventures geographic and military, including the Guiana Voyage of 1595, the Azores Voyage

Sir Walter Ralegh
Nicholas Hilliard, c.1585
This brilliant Hilliard miniature is the first
portrait of Ralegh. With his dark, sultry
looks and pearls and lace in abundance,
he is the court dandy epitomised.

of 1597 (with John Donne among the company) and the action
at Cádiz. He was also a vigorous speaker in Parliament.

Ralegh was a compelling but curtailed figure during the
last years of Elizabeth: he regained some power but not her full
confidence. In 1603 his star fell once more. Embroiled in conspiracy
against the new King James, he was dispatched to the Tower under
sentence of death. He remained there thirteen years, writing his
History of the World, brewing his alchemical distillations in a converted
henhouse in the Tower gardens and petitioning for a last chance to
find the fabled gold of Guiana. His wish was granted in 1617, but
the expedition was a disaster, resulting in the suicide of his faithful
servant Laurence Keymis and the death of his son Wat. A newsletter
brought back by one of the voyagers, Peter Alley, has a woodcut
portrait of Ralegh: a bleak, sunken-eyed image. On his return to
England, the old treason charge was revived and Ralegh was executed
in Old Palace Yard, Westminster, in September 1618. His head was
placed in a red velvet bag and was kept by his widow until her death
in the 1630s. It is said to lie beneath a concrete floor in the church
of West Horsley, Surrey, where his youngest son, Carew, is buried.

NEVVES
Of S^r. VValter Rauleigh.

WITH
The true Defcription of GVIANA:

As alfo a Relation of the excellent Gouernment, and much hope of the profperity of the Voyage.

Sent from a Gentleman of his Fleet, to a moft efpeciall Friend of his in London.

From the Riuer of Caliana, *on the Coaft of* Guiana, *Nouemb.* 17. 1617.

LONDON,
Printed for *H. G.* and are to be fold by *I. Wright*, at the figne of the Bible without New-gate. 1618.

This full-length portrait with his second son, Wat, shows Ralegh in a white silk doublet and a pearl-embroidered jacket, but the allure of the portrait lies in its quiet dignity, its sense of his personal strength amid disappointments, and the poignant optimism of the young boy beside him. Wat (who was for a while tutored by Ben Jonson, and was to die on Ralegh's last voyage to South America, in 1618) is eight years old here.

Patrons

Patronage was an accepted fact of the Elizabethan literary world. The relationship varied: a patron might be the writer's friend, or his employer (the writer working as secretary or tutor, for example), or just the giver of occasional 'liberalities' and 'doles' that kept the wolf from the door. At its most functional, the patron simply paid a 'dedication fee' – typically £2 – in return for a lavish encomium at the beginning of a book. The theatrical companies also depended on patronage: they wore their patron's livery and performed under his or her nominal protection.

The patronage system may seem archaic and demeaning today, and certainly some writers at the time resented the servitude – Nashe speaks bitterly of penning 'toys for private gentlemen' and of the wasted hours hanging around in the ante-chambers of 'Lord What-call-ye-him' – but it remains true that the glories of Elizabethan literature were made possible by the generosity and encouragement of a few rich and influential figures.

Henry Wriothesley, 3rd Earl of Southampton (1573–1624), is perhaps the best-known of Elizabethan patrons due to his close association with Shakespeare, who dedicated *Venus and Adonis* (1593) and *Lucrece* (1594) to him. The tone of the first dedication is formulaic, the second more personal: 'What I have done is yours, what I have to do is yours, being part in all I have, devoted yours'. Southampton was then twenty years old, a wayward young aristocrat with wavering Catholic sympathies. He was also a very eligible bachelor whom Lord Burghley, his guardian, was keen to marry off to Elizabeth de Vere, daughter of the Earl of Oxford (see page 89). This may tie in with the opening sequence of Shakespeare's *Sonnets*, which is on the theme of marriage. It is certainly a good guess, if no more,

....
**Henry Wriothesley,
3rd Earl of Southampton**
Unknown artist, c.1600
Henry Wriothesley's striking, almost feline, looks and his flowing auburn hair (worn much longer than fashion dictated) are displayed in this fine full-length portrait, on loan to the National Portrait Gallery from a private collection. It is dated by costume to c.1595–1600, the helmet and breastplate might suggest a date around 1596, when he took part in the naval attack on Cádiz.

that Southampton is the 'fair youth' addressed in the Sonnets, and that the relationship between patron and poet was close.

During the naval assault on Cádiz in 1596, and in much else, Southampton was a follower of the Earl of Essex, and he was deeply implicated in the 1601 Rising (see page 10). His death sentence was commuted to life-imprisonment, but he had served less than two years when the new King James released him and reinstated his earldom. His later life was morally upright: he was active in colonial ventures, becoming Treasurer of the Virginia Company in 1620, and he fought in the Netherlands, where he died of a fever, at Bergen-op-Zoom, in 1624.

Sir George Carey, 2nd Lord Hunsdon (1547–1603), was nominated Lord Chamberlain in 1597 and thus became the patron

Sir George Carey, 2nd Lord Hunsdon
Nicholas Hilliard, 1601
This miniature by Hilliard shows Carey at the age of fifty-four, two years before his death from syphilis. A ditty of the day referred to his sexual adventures: 'Chamberlain, Chamberlain, he's of her Grace's kin/Fool hath he ever been with his Joan Silverpin.'

of Shakespeare's theatre company, the Lord Chamberlain's Men. The troupe had been formed three years earlier under the patronage of his father, Henry, 1st Lord Hunsdon. (This elder Hunsdon had a half-Italian mistress, Emilia Bassano, who is thought by some to be the 'Dark Lady' of Shakespeare's *Sonnets*.) The first performance of *The Merry Wives of Windsor* was in all likelihood given in Carey's honour, when he was invested with the Order of the Garter, at Windsor, in March 1597.

Carey was a generous patron who, in the words of George Chapman, gave 'vital warmth to freezing science'. Thomas Nashe found shelter as his guest at Carisbrooke Castle on the Isle of Wight (Carey was governor of the island) and later said of him:

Whatsoever minute's intermission I have of calmed content proceedeth from him. Through him my tender wainscot study door is delivered from much assault and battery. Through him I look into and am looked on in the world, from whence otherwise I were a wretched banished exile. (*Terrors of the Night*, 1594)

Carey was also a patron of the composer John Dowland, who dedicated his *First Book of Songs and Airs* (1597) to him, and of the astrologer-physician Simon Forman.

The talented and popular **Ferdinando Stanley, 5th Earl of Derby** (c.1558–94), was known as Lord Strange until his accession to the earldom on the death of his father in 1593. His theatre troupe, Strange's Men, was the leading company of the early 1590s and formed the nucleus of the Lord Chamberlain's Men. Strange's Men performed Shakespeare's *Henry VI Part One* and Marlowe's *The Jew of Malta* at the Rose theatre in 1592. Under arrest in the Netherlands, Marlowe stated he was 'very well-known' to Lord Strange. Thomas Kyd confirms this connection, but adds that Strange 'could not endure' Marlowe once 'he learned of his conditions' (i.e. as an atheist).

Strange's circle was scholarly and occultist – Shakespeare may be gently satirising it as the 'little academe' of philosophers in *Love's Labours Lost* – but he is also the 'Lord S' for whom Thomas Nashe wrote his bawdy doggerel poem 'The Choice of Valentines', popularly known as 'Nashe's Dildo'. Other writers who praised Strange are George Chapman, Matthew Roydon and Edmund Spenser (see pages 76–7), who was a kinsman of Strange's wife, Alice née Spenser. Strange was himself a poet who, in Spenser's words, 'could pipe with passing skill'; some of his poems appeared in the popular anthology *Belvedere* (1600).

From a Catholic-leaning family, and blood-related to the Queen on both sides of his family, Strange was bedevilled by Catholic plotters trying to persuade him into the role of pretender to the throne. One such persuader, Richard Hesketh, was hanged in 1593. Six months later, Strange died in great pain, at his house in Lathom, Lancashire. He believed he was the victim of witchcraft, but the symptoms suggest poison.

William Herbert, 3rd Earl of Pembroke (1580–1930), the eldest son of Mary Sidney, was named by the editors of the First Folio as a patron who had shown 'much favour' to Shakespeare.

Some would make him, rather than Southampton, the addressee of the *Sonnets*, and even the 'Mr W.H.' described in the first edition of 1609 as their 'only begetter' (though most Elizabethan publishers knew better than to address an Earl as 'Mr'). He was 'immoderately given up to women', but after his talk-of-the-town affairs with Mal Fitton (see page 94) and his cousin Mary Wroth, he succumbed to an unhappy, childless marriage to Lady Mary Talbot, co-heiress to the Earl of Shrewsbury. Herbert is described by Anthony Wood as 'the very picture and *vera effigies* of nobility'.

....

William Herbert, 3rd Earl of Pembroke

after Daniel Mytens, c.1625

This magisterial full-length portrait shows Herbert with the white rod of the Lord Chamberlain's office, to which he was appointed in 1615, but the country-house background suggests a more private kind of stateliness: a vision of the elegance, order and prosperity that the patron offered, symbolically at least, to the hard-pressed writer.

SELECT BIBLIOGRAPHY

Aubrey, John, *Brief Lives*, ed. Oliver Lawson Dick (Secker & Warburg, London, 1950)

Black, J.B., *The Reign of Elizabeth 1558–1603* (Clarendon Press, Oxford, 1959)

Birch, Thomas, *Memoirs of the Reign of Queen Elizabeth*, 3 vols (A. Millar, London, 1754)

Cooper, Tarnya, *Searching for Shakespeare* (exh. cat. National Portrait Gallery, London, 2006)

Cust, L., 'The Portraits of Sir Walter Raleigh', *Walpole Society*, VIII, 1920, pp.6–7

Donaldson, Ian, *Ben Jonson: A Life* (Oxford University Press, Oxford, 2011)

Duncan-Jones, Katherine, *Ungentle Shakespeare: Scenes from his life* (Arden Shakespeare, London, 2001)

Eccles, Mark, 'Brief Lives: Tudor and Stuart Authors', *Studies in Philology*, 79, 1982

Edmond, Mary, 'The Chandos Portrait: A Suggested Painter', *Burlington Magazine*, vol.CXXIX, 1982, pp.146–9
     'It was for Gentle Shakespeare Out' (*Shakespeare Quarterly*, vol. 43, 1991, pp.339–44)

Fraser, Antonia, *The Gunpowder Plot: Terror and Faith in 1605* (Weidenfeld & Nicolson, London, 1996)

Fuller, Thomas, *The History of the Worthies of England* (London, 1662)

Gent, Lucy, *Picture and Poetry 1560–1620: Relations Between Literature and the Visual Arts in the English Renaissance* (J. Hall, Leamington Spa, 1981)

Goulding, R.W., 'Wriothesley Portraits', *Walpole Society*, VIII, 1920, pp.51–62

Gurr, Andrew, *Playgoing in Shakespeare's London* (Cambridge University Press, Cambridge, 1987)

Hadfield, Andrew, *Edmund Spenser: A Life* (Oxford University Press, Oxford, 2012)

Haynes, Alan, *Robert Cecil, 1st Earl of Salisbury* (Peter Owen, London, 1989)
     Sex in Elizabethan England (Sutton Publishing, Stroud, 1997)

Henslowe, Philip, *Diary*, eds R.A. Foakes and R.T. Rickert (Cambridge University Press, Cambridge, 1961)

Honan, Park, *Shakespeare: A Life* (Clarendon Press, Oxford, 1998)

Kelsey, Harry, *Sir Francis Drake: The Queen's Pirate* (Yale University Press, London, 1998)

Knights, L.C., *Drama and Society in the Age of Jonson* (Chatto & Windus, London, 1937)

Mathews, Nieves, *Francis Bacon: The History of a Character Assassination* (Yale University Press, London, 1996)

Miller, Edwin H., *The Professional Writer in Elizabethan England* (Harvard University Press, Cambridge, Mass., 1959)

Nicholl, Charles, *A Cup of News: The Life of Thomas Nashe* (Routledge, London, 1984)
     The Reckoning: The Murder of Christopher Marlowe (Jonathan Cape, London, 1992; revised edition 2002)
     The Lodger: Shakespeare on Silver Street (Allen Lane, London, 2007)

Picard, Liza, *Elizabeth's London* (Weidenfeld & Nicolson, London, 2003)

Rhodes, Neil, *Elizabethan Grotesque* (Routledge, London, 1980)

Riggs, David, *Ben Jonson: A Life* (Harvard University Press, Cambridge, Mass., 1989)
     The World of Christopher Marlowe (Faber & Faber, London, 2004)

Schoenbaum, Samuel, *Shakespeare: A Documentary Life* (Oxford University Press, Oxford, 1975; revised edition 1987)

Shapiro, James, *1599: A Year in the Life of William Shakespeare* (Faber & Faber, London, 2005)

Sheavyn, Phoebe, *The Literary Profession in the Elizabethan Age* (Manchester University Press, Manchester, 1967)

Stewart, Alan, *Sir Philip Sidney: A Double Life* (Chatto & Windus, London, 2000)
     The Cradle King: A Life of James VI and I (Chatto & Windus, London, 2003)

Strachey, Lytton, *Elizabeth and Essex* (Chatto & Windus, London, 1928)

Strong, Roy, 'The Leicester House Miniatures: Robert Sidney, 1st Earl of Leicester and his Circle', *Burlington Magazine*, vol.CXXVII, 1985, pp.694–701

Strype, John, *Annals of the Reformation*, 4 vols (Oxford, 1824)

Stow, John, *A Survey of London*, ed. C.L. Kingsford, 2 vols (Oxford, 1908)

Woolley, Benjamin, *The Queen's Conjuror: The Science and Magic of Dr John Dee* (HarperCollins, London, 2001)

LIST OF ILLUSTRATIONS

INDEX

Note: page numbers in **bold** refer to captions.